C. WRIGHT MILLS

KEY SOCIOLOGISTS
Series Editor: Peter Hamilton
The Open University

KEY SOCIOLOGISTS

Series Editor: PETER HAMILTON
The Open University, Milton Keynes

This series will present concise and readable texts covering the work, life and influence of many of the most important sociologists, and sociologically-relevant thinkers, from the birth of the discipline to the present day. Aimed primarily at the undergraduate, the books will also be useful to pre-university students and others who are interested in the main ideas of sociology's major thinkers.

MARX and Marxism
PETER WORSLEY
Professor of Sociology, University of Manchester

MAX WEBER
FRANK PARKIN
Tutor in Politics and Fellow of Magdalen College, Oxford

EMILE DURKHEIM
KENNETH THOMPSON
Reader in Sociology, Faculty of Social Sciences, The Open University, Milton Keynes

TALCOTT PARSONS
PETER HAMILTON
The Open University, Milton Keynes

SIGMUND FREUD
ROBERT BOCOCK
The Open University, Milton Keynes

THE FRANKFURT SCHOOL
TOM BOTTOMORE
Professor of Sociology, University of Sussex

C. WRIGHT MILLS
JOHN ELDRIDGE
Professor of Sociology, University of Glasgow

GEORG SIMMEL
DAVID FRISBY
Department of Sociology, University of Glasgow

C. WRIGHT MILLS

J. E. T. ELDRIDGE
Professor of Sociology
University of Glasgow

ELLIS HORWOOD LIMITED
Publishers · Chichester

TAVISTOCK PUBLICATIONS
London and New York

First published in 1983 by
ELLIS HORWOOD LIMITED
Market Cross House, Cooper Street
Chichester, Sussex, PO19 1EB, England

and

TAVISTOCK PUBLICATIONS LIMITED
11 New Fetter Lane, London EC4P 4EE

Published in the USA by
TAVISTOCK PUBLICATIONS
and ELLIS HORWOOD LIMITED
in association with METHUEN INC.
733 Third Avenue, New York, NY 10017

British Library Cataloguing in Publication Data
Eldridge, J. E. T.
C. Wright Mills. — (Key sociologists)
1. Mills, C. Wright — Sociology
I. Title   II. Series
301'.092'4   HM22.U6

Library of Congress Card No. 82–25480

ISBN 0-85312-533-3 (Ellis Horwood Ltd., Publishers — Library Edn.)
ISBN 0-85312-534-1 (Ellis Horwood Ltd., Publishers — Student Edn.)
Typeset in Press Roman by Ellis Horwood Ltd.
Printed in Great Britain by R. J. Acford, Chichester.

Table of Contents

Editor's Foreword

Charles Wright Mills stands in a rather special relation to mainstream sociology. Although his working life as a sociologist was comparatively brief — a little over twenty years in all — his impact on the discipline was disproportionately great. Yet Mills was not a popular figure amongst many of his fellow sociologists, especially after he began to publish polemical studies of the unacceptable face of American society during the 'end of ideology' 1950s. Edward Shils even referred to him as 'in part a rough-tongued brawler', perhaps a view of Mills shared by many in the American establishment who may have found his critical essays on power in American society, and the USA's domination of Caribbean affairs, difficult to swallow. As a maverick sociologist he also clearly irritated a number of his peers by his overwhelming interest in criticizing the prevailing sociological orthodoxy — in reducing, for example, much of Talcott Parsons's carefully argued analytical theory of the *Social System* to a few trivial commonsense points. Such jibes were never likely, or designed, to endear him to his colleagues.

But Mills was not just a cynical critic of sociology, or a closet Marxist chipping away at the foundations of American society. In fact he stands directly in a long tradition of social criticism and political dissent which has deep roots in American culture. Mills may be seen as an intellectual representative of Midwestern populism, an egalitarian political philosophy which has its sources in the small towns and cities of North America, and which is characterized by a distrust of big government and big business, preferring local to cosmopolitan values, and stressing the virtues of pragmatism against arid intellectualism. Although populism spawned such figures as Joe McCarthy, and is as a result often portrayed misleadingly as a fundamentally conservative ideology, it is much better understood as a popular democratic philosophy of 'small is beautiful' opposed to all forms of hegemonic domination of local and small-scale communities by large state institutions, bureaucratic religions or business monopolies. It has close links to the philosophical position termed *pragmatism* elaborated by Peirce, James, Dewey and G. H. Mead, and indeed Mills considered himself firmly located in that tradition of thought with its emphases on the union of the practical and the intellectual which is symbolized in his notion of the sociologist as a sort of 'cultural workman'.

The pragmatists believed that intellectuals should be involved and interested in practical affairs, not cut off from them by academicism and isolation in ivory tower universities. Mills exemplifies both the populist and pragmatist traditions — throughout his life he wrote for a wide range of audiences, from the narrowly intellectual to the most popular, and was always insistent on the need for the sociologist to be unafraid of getting his hands dirty in practical affairs. Yet he was also a considerable scholar, the co-editor of the first major selection of Weber's work to be made available in English. His writings on the sociology of knowledge, and on social psychology (with Hans Gerth), are notable contributions to the literature of these two fields.

J. E. T. Eldridge's study of Mills is a most timely work, for it provides us for the first time with a concise and sympathetic evaluation of the whole of his work. Views of Mills's contribution to sociology tend to overemphasize his best-known work — *The Sociological Imagination, The Power Elite* and *White Collar* — at the expense of the lesser-known pieces, many of which are equally impressive as examples of the cultural workman's trade. Professor Eldridge shows us how Mills's radical pragmatism and essential populism were increasingly pervaded by a Marxist humanism which supported his critical stance *vis-à-vis* sociological orthodoxy, and informed his assessments of the main social and political issues of his day. Mills was in many ways the ideal 'radical' or committed sociologist, as those terms are understood in American sociology. Indeed much of his lasting appeal is precisely to those whose image of sociology is of a liberating discipline whose role is to act on behalf of public interests in the criticism of social structures and institutions. Although an important element of Mills's work consists of just such a 'critical sociology' to stop at that point would give a one sided impression of Mills's achievement. Through Professor Eldridge's assessment of Mills we can clearly begin to see the multidimensional character of his work, and to recognize that his claim to the status of 'key' sociologist rests on more than acerbic polemic.

Peter Hamilton

For
Paul, Elizabeth and Alison

JOHN ELDRIDGE is Professor of Sociology in the
University of Glasgow, a position he has held since
1972. He is a founder member of the Glasgow
University Media Group and of the Centre for
Research in Industrial Democracy and Participation,
at the same University. He is current Chairman of the
recently-formed Association for Learned Societies in
the Social Sciences.

Acknowledgements

I am responsible for the opinions expressed in this text. A number of people have helped me in the course of my work and I should like to thank them warmly. They are Rosemary Eldridge, Robert Farr, David Frisby, Ralph Miliband and Hillel Ticktin. My thanks too for the friendly support from the editor of this series Peter Hamilton.

1

The Making of a Cultural Workman

1.1 INTRODUCTION

When Charles Wright Mills died in 1962 at the age of forty-five, he was reputed to be the most widely read sociologist in the world. His work was marked by vigour and energy. He challenged much that passed for conventional wisdom in the spheres of politics and sociology. He became, in what is nearly always an ambiguous phrase, a controversial figure. Irving Horowitz has conveyed something of the flavour of this:

> During his lifetime and after, Mills was accused by some of being a Manichean, by others as a Machiavellian, and by yet others as a Marxian. He was racked for being a thinker saturated with a love of power, and at the same time criticized for his super-intellectualism, his idealistic disregard of real factors of power such as the economic system ... It seems to be the fate of significant figures that the size and extent of the caricature to which they are subjected is itself an inadvertent accolade.

Was he a populist? Was he a Trotskyist? No doubt he was sometimes tempted to join in the game of who he was supposed to be as when he described his self-appointed task as being 'simultaneously a Teddy Roosevelt and an F. Scott Fitzgerald, a public figure — a man of action and an artist-thinker' [2].

In this book we will offer an account and assessment of Mills's work. There are two main elements in our approach. The first is to discuss the intellectual influences upon Mills and his response to them. Broadly these will be traced through his academic career from Texas to Columbia and will convey some sense of the intellectual milieu to which he was exposed. Secondly, we will give a critical exposition of Mills's major works. Despite the fact that much of his work was widely disseminated, more particularly by means of the paperback revolution, not all of it is equally well known. Only by an overview of the totality of his major publications can we hope to make a reasonable assessment. We began with the thought that any man who caused as much 'troubling of the waters' as he did must have something going for him. Despite a number of critical caveats we were not disappointed and in these pages will hope to explain why.

1.2 FROM TEXAS TO WISCONSIN

From 1916 to 1939 Mills lived in Texas, growing up in Sherman, Fort Worth and Dallas and changing schools a good number of times in the process. He was born into a middle class Catholic family. There is one element about this family background which has been referred to by Richard Gillam. He suggests that the writing of *White Collar* has a strongly autobiographical aspect to it.

> Mills conceded that his gloomy account of decline from propertied autonomy to salaried independence — from farm or ranch to office — recapitulated family history. In *White Collar* he sees 'heroes' like a larger-than-life maternal grandfather (Braxton Bragg Wright), killed in a gunfight on his Texas cattle ranch, giving way to 'victims' like his insurance-agent father (Charles Grover Mills, or 'G,C.' to his son) and status-driven mother. So a generational metamorphosis as exemplified in the contrast between Braxton Bragg and C.G. becomes virtually emblematic of America as a whole. Bitter memories of an unhappy boyhood also color a self-referential description of 'lumpen-bourgeois' children as 'objects upon which parental frustrations are projected ... subjected alternately to over-indulgence ... and to strong discipline ... based on the parents' urge to 'make the child amount to something'. This was nothing less than the early experience of 'Charleswright' — his mother's spoiled favourite — writ large. [3]

From various sources the impression is gleaned of an unhappy childhood. As a young man he was sent to a rural military school — Texas A. and M. — 'to make a man of him' as his father put it. This proved to be a miserable time — although, given his later sociological interest in the military, there may have been some unexpected long-term benefits. After a year he was permitted to transfer to the University of Texas at Austin. There his intellectual faculties were really stimulated and his academic pilgrimage began [4].

At Texas he read philosophy. His teachers included Clarence Ayers, a former associate of Thorstein Veblen, and George Gentry, who had studied under G. H. Mead and who introduced Mills to the writings of the pragmatist philosophers. All of this, as we shall see, turned out to be of considerable relevance for Mills's later work and interests.

Mills came to the settled view that Veblen was the best social scientist America had produced [5]. He came to admire him as a social critic and as a theorist who had learned something from Marx, which he had applied in a distinctive way to American society. If we bring to mind some of Veblen's major books — *The Theory of the Leisure Class, The Theory of the Business Enterprise, Instinct of Workmanship, The Nature of Peace, The Higher Learning, Absentee Ownership* — we can see that the kinds of issues he addressed often concerned contemporary problems in American society and the kind of ground covered was really very similar to the subjects tackled by Mills several decades later. Mills saw in Veblen an intellectual craftsman whose work could serve as a worthy model for the apprentice social scientist.

In 1953, Mills wrote an introduction to the paperback edition of *The Theory of the Leisure Class,* where he described Veblen's work as having real and lasting value: '... he opens up our minds, he gets us "outside the whale", he makes us see through the official sham. Above all, he teaches us to be aware of the crackpot basis of the realism of those practical Men of Affairs who would lead us to honorific destruction'. [6] One of the concepts Mills was to deploy in a great deal of his writing is that of 'drift' or 'the main drift', and this is derivative of Veblen. Drift describes social changes that take place but which are not always visible to the general public until they are far advanced. These changes occur, as it were, behind our backs and in any case tend to be hidden from us by the rhetoric and verbiage of public life. One such example was the drift of circumstances surrounding the growth of absentee ownership. Behind all the political talk of patriotism, the common good and democracy was the substantial fact of the economic shift in patterns of ownership. Yet what is actually represented were threats to democratic politics and the growth of economic inequalities.

Mills, no doubt, liked the way in which Veblen identified conflicts of interest — sometimes latent, sometimes manifest, but always present — in society. In the process Veblen would also identify some of the paradoxes that could be entailed. For example, big business — characterized by a absentee ownership — was always talking the language of efficiency and practicality. Veblen was convinced that it did not live up to these claims. In particular the relations between capital and labour were marked by mutual mistrust and sharp practice. This was a way for inefficiency and was not a practical way to conduct national affairs. Again, business interests become equated with national interests and yet there is a camouflaging activity that hides the precise nature of this equation. The idea that this camouflage can be stripped away to reveal what is actually going on is something that Mills appreciates in Veblen's ironic salvoes.

Veblen sought to make wide connections in his social analysis: cultural symbols, the role of religion and military activity could be related to comments on international trade and foreign policy. Consider how he writes about imperialism, or what he suggested might equally well be called 'the national graft', to an American audience. He writes of the way in which trade and financial interests work with the help of government and do business in foreign parts:

All the while, of course, this trading on the national integrity is carried on as inconspicuously as may be, quite legally and morally under democratic forms, by night and cloud, and is covered over with as much decently voluble prevarication as the case may require, prevarication of a decently statesmanlike sort; such a volume and texture of prevarication as may serve to keep the national left hand from knowing what the right hand is doing, the left hand in these premises being the community at large, as contrasted with the Interests and the official personnel. In all such work of administrative prevarication and democratic camouflage the statesmen are greatly helped out by the newspapers and the approved agencies that gather and purvey such news as is fit to print for the purposes in hand. The pulpit, too, has its expedient uses as a publicity agency in furtherance of the gainful pursuit of national enterprise in foreign parts. [7]

The critic, of course, is liable to be in a difficult position. There is the difficulty of convincing the public at large of what takes place, as it were, under cover of darkness. Moreover, to question business interests is to question the national interest and that is likely to be treated as subversive and seditious behaviour and certainly as unpatriotic: 'Any pronounced degree of scepticism touching the expediency of any of the accomplished facts of political intrigue or administrative control is due to be penalised as obnoxious to the common good' [8]. Yet the critic may speak as one who sees the common good eroded and threatened by the rhetoric which purports to sustain it. Only as the reality of the main drift of events is understood can the values which particular and dominant interests represent be consciously appraised. This is a prerequisite for a truly democratic society. Mills shared with Veblen this view of the close relationship between social analysis and social criticism. Like Veblen his work was to be wide ranging, sometimes directed at the academic audience and sometimes through journalism and radical pamphlets at a much wider audience. Even those who came to take a hostile stance towards Mills were sometimes willing to concede that he was something of a latter-day Veblen.

Mills's debt and response to pragmatatism, notably the works of Peirce, Mead, William James and Dewey, will be made clearer as we proceed. At this point we simply wish to draw attention to some remarks by Irving Horowitz on the significance of William James who, along with Veblen, was much admired by Mills:

> From his first efforts, to his last unpublished writings, C. Wright Mills retained a lively interest in the social and intellectual values of pragmatism. He was the embodiment of Jamesian Man; complete with a heroic definition of self. Like William James he invested in political beliefs with a highly personal content. He inveighed against American intervention in Latin America quite in the same way, and with the same motives, as James's activities in the Anti-Imperialist League. His faith in intellectual activity as a way out of the morass of power was articulated in a manner made famous in Jame's words: 'Les intellectuels unite!' At the same time, Mills's mistrust of narrow professionalism sounds a familiar note to those acquainted with Mills's indictment of the higher academicisms. The similarities between Mills and James are so patently clear, it is disconcerting to see how thoroughly the connection has been missed. [9]

Mills was to advance some criticisms of James as we shall see. Temperamentally too he was more of a pessimist, when set against James's normally cheerful spirit. But Horowitz is right to emphasize the strong affinities between the two.

When Mills went to Wisconsin as a graduate student in 1939 Edward A. Ross, who founded the Department of Sociology there was still Head of Department. Mills held him in high regard. Even in one of his last books, *The Sociological Imagination,* Ross is cited as a classic social analyst, 'graceful, muckraking, upright' [10]. Muckrakers in the American tradition were crusading liberals who challenged big monopolies — banks, businesses and trade unions. In *Sociology and Pragmatism,* a revised version of his doctoral thesis written while he was at Wisconsin, Mills refers to Ross explicitly:

> In the heyday of 'progressive crusading' E. A. Ross refracted muckraking in academic terms. He stood for the farmer as an individual. He fought the big monopolies and since he was regionally West, he especially fought the railroads. What he stood for was Jeffersonism. In 1907 he translated the issues arising out of the struggles of farmers and small businessmen versus Big Businessmen into the moral vocabulary of the Jeffersonian world. 'Tax-dodging is larceny ... railroad discrimination is treachery ... Embezzlement is theft'. [11]

Ross's individualism was an intellectual response to the drift from a rural to an urban society. Jeffersonianism remained an important bench mark for Mills even though he knew that the clock could never be turned back. He also steadfastly maintained a dislike of big business, coupled sometimes with a horrified fascination with it. Clearly he accepted the right of the social scientist to use a moral vocabulary and himself sought to deploy one that would have contemporary relevance.

In *Character and Social Structure* Gerth and Mills refer to Ross in the company of such as Karl Mannheim and Ortega Y. Gasset for his discussion of mass society and cite his 'great books' *Social Control* (1904) and *Social Psychology* (1908).

Ross, no doubt, would have taken pleasure in a report which Mills was to prepare in 1946 for a US Senate Special Committee to Study Problems of American Small Business — *Small Business and Civic Welfare.* Based on three pairs of cities matched for geographical location, population size and ethnic composition, the study concluded that it was in small-business cities where the most favourable environment for the development and growth of civic spirit could be found. Mills used Thorndike's G score (G for Goodness) which sought to embrace and codify indices on health, education, recreation, economy, social facilities and public utilities. Besides producing statistical data to show that in small-business cities employment fluctuations are less, the quality of retail services better, public health better, distribution of income more equitable, Mills went on to criticize big business. The power of these absentee-owned firms in the community does not usually arise from a direct contribution to civic affairs. They have power of life or death over the economic life of the town, their threat to leave is a very strong weapon and this serves as a veto on local decisions of which they disapprove. They can exercise influence surreptitiously behind the facade of local puppets who do their bidding. For Mills this portrait is a version of small is beautiful and we can also see shades of Veblen in it. If the rural drift could not be stopped perhaps policy could be directed towards creating more balanced city economies in which small businesses were much in evidence.

At Wisconsin, Mills met Hans Gerth, who was first his teacher and then his collaborator in scholarly work. Gerth had been a student at the Frankfurt Institute for Social Research. When he left Nazi Germany he brought with him to Wisconsin a deep knowledge of European social thought and a strong interest in comparative studies. According to Scimecca, Mills did not read Marx until the mid-1950s [12]. Bearing in mind his early association with Gerth and the internal evidence from his own work it is difficult to see how such a view can be sustained. Through Gerth the works of Marx, Weber and Mannheim (one of Gerth's teachers at Frankfurt) had been mediated to Mills. Here the young philosophy student from Texas with his strong interest in the American pragmatist tradition was encouraged to develop a sociological perspective. The mix of the two was to denote the distinctive Mills approach to social analysis in the years that followed. Indeed, his first published work, 'Language, Logic and Culture', which appeared in the *American Sociological Review* in 1939 contained explicit references to the pragmatists, Peirce, Dewey and Mead on the one hand and to Marx and Mannheim on the other, with a glancing reference to Weber by by way of Talcott Parsons's newly published *Structure of Social Action* (1939).

In the period 1939-40 Mills, still only in his early twenties, had three articles published which were stimulating contributions to the sociology of knowledge. They still merit attention and we will consider them briefly here. 'Language, Logic and Culture' asks: what are the relationships between a thinker and his or her social context? Mills conveys his dissatisfaction with Marxist attempts to relate ideas to social structure because, he claims, terms like 'reflect', 'mould', 'determine', or 'penetrate' are question-begging and hide inadequate analysis. Mannheim also is criticized for his vague and unanalysed use of the term collective unconscious' in *Ideology and Utopia*.

Mills makes two suggestions for moving the debate on. The first is to make modified use of G. H. Mead's concept of 'the generalized other' to show how societal processes enter as determinants on reflection. The generalized other is not deployed, as in Mead, to stand for 'the whole society' but for selected segments of it, namely the social audience with whom the thinker interacts. Thought is conversation with an audience characterized by certain social and intellectual habits and the interaction involves experience of recalcitrance, rejection, reformulation and acceptance. What counts as logical argument or validation of a position? Mills claims that these are conventional but not arbitrary matters. They are relative to particular epochs and cultures. In this social theory of mind the generalized other is involved in the functioning and conditioning of the outcome of reflection. It thereby shapes the logical apparatus and the way it is deployed.

Mills's second suggestion is to focus on language as mediating between mind and society. The nub of the argument is put in this way:

> Symbols are the 'directing pivots' of social behaviour. They are also the indispensable condition of human mentality. The meanings of words are formed and sustained by the interactions of human collectivities, and thought as the manipulation of such meanings. Mind is the interplay of the organism with social situations mediated by symbols. The patterns of social behaviour with their 'cultural drifts' and values, and political orientations extend a control over thought by means of language. It is only by utilising the symbols common to this group that a thinker can think and communicate. [13]

Hence different cultures have different vocabularies and different modes of thought. And within a society a vocabulary may be located within different institutional and political co-ordinates. This helps to explain why different groups in society sometimes 'talk past each other': the vocabulary is either not mutually understood — it may be 'incomprehensible' to some ears — or decoded by some hearers to mean something quite different to what the communicator intended.

In 'Methodological consequences of the Sociology of Knowledge' Mills's relativist perspective is again evident. His view is that the sociology of knowledge has epistemological consequences because models or systems of empirical verification are themselves socially formed. They are not transcendental. Truth and objectivity, dependent as they are on social contexts that have different criteria for establishing them, are necessarily relative. 'He who asserts the irrelevance of social conditions to the truthfulness of the propositions ought to state the conditions upon which he conceives truthfulness actually to depend; he ought to specify exactly what it is in thinking that sociological factors cannot explain and upon which truth and validity do rest' [14]. Mills sees Dewey and Mannheim as agreeing on this point though coming to it by different routes. Again, language is crucial to the issues: 'Empirical verification cannot be a simple and positivist, mirror-like operation. Thus the observational dimensions of any verificatory model are influenced by the selective language of its users. And this language is not without social-historical imprint' [15].

When the sociologist of knowledge draws attention to such things, then absolutist theories of truth are challenged, since objectivity and impartiality are themselves treated as cultural artefacts. One of the tasks of the sociology of knowledge, on this reckoning, is to study the epistemological diversity of verification models and the social context in which they flourish. In other words, a comparative study of knowledge paradigms is advocated. This could involve comparisons between social science and natural science forms of enquiry. Perhaps, suggests Mills, the natural science form of enquiry can be shown to be inadequate for social science investigations. Again, the sociology of knowledge might detect, more rigorously, how value questions permeate social investigations. How do they condition the direction, completeness and warrantability of research findings? The sociologist of knowledge is a crucial and critical guide. Mills concludes on a hopeful note: 'The detailed self-location of social science, if systematically and sensitively performed, not only will lead to detection of errors in methods under way but constructively will result in the presentation of sounder paradigms for future research' [16].

How does Mills seek to escape the relativist's dilemma? He takes the view that all truth is conditional, not absolute, and that a sociology of knowledge speaks only of probabilities. Reflection on social enquiry, makes possible the correction of the social sources of error and might lead to the development of new criteria for social science. There is, in other words, a corrective function based on an exploration and critique of existing models of verification and clarifying the social context in which they operate. Mills endorses Mannheim's distinction between relativism and relationism as a way out of the dilemma. Will this do?

One of the few writers to discuss Mills's sociology of knowledge is Derek L. Phillips, whose paper 'Epistemology and the Sociology of Knowledge', considers the contributions of Mannheim, Mills and Merton [17]. He points out that the radically social view of the nature of logic and reasoning anticipates the current controversies surrounding the work of Thomas Kuhn's *The Structure of Scientific Revolutions* [18]. However, he questions whether the distinction between relativism and relationism in Mannheim and Mills is an adequate response to the absolutist's challenge. To say that we must look at the social structure in which intellectual phenomena emerged, in order to comment on their validity, presupposes a method for obtaining knowledge of social structures. How is that knowledge to be evaluated? The relativist's dilemma is not solved by recourse to relationism: either the relativists' own assertions are relative and therefore lacking in truth value; or they are unconditionally true and therefore relativism is self-contradictory.

This remains an intellectual and personal problem for Mills, not least since, in his later writings, he advocates the 'politics of truth'. Like Mannheim, he came to formulate a critical role in public life for the intellectual. We hazard the conjecture that some of his more strident outbursts were a matter of shouting louder because he realized that his epistemological position could compromise the prophetic utterance. In recent years, essays by Ernest Gellner and Steven Lukes have indicated possible solutions to the relativist's dilemma that Mills might have found convincing, but we do no more here than draw attention to them [19].

The third paper, 'Situated Actions and Vocabularies of Motives' was subsequently to be incorporated into *Character and Social Structure,* which we discuss later. Suffice it to say that it was a seminal article with its radically sociological view of motivation, rejecting reductionism, whether practiced in the name of Marx or Freud. We see in the paper how Mills elaborates a typology of vocabularies: religious, hedonistic, sexual, moral, economic. In particular, we can observe the pragmatic perspective in Mills encountering Weber's treatment of motivation and recognizing the intrinsically social character of both treatments. Motives for Mills, as for Weber, are accepted justifications for present, future or past programmes or acts [20]. This we take as our cue to turn to the influence of Weber on Mills.

Gerth had translated a number of Weber's essays. Mills had polished up the English style. Together they wrote an introduction to the book and the justly celebrated collection *From Max Weber,* was eventually published in 1946. Gerth has recorded that Mills loved working at the Weber materials [21].

Of all the European social theorists Weber stands out as the dominant influence on Mills. Some of the reasons are not hard to see. Weber, the liberal, tracing out the processes of bureaucratization and rationalization, identifying the emergence of high capitalism and state socialism displays 'a defensive pessimism for the future of freedom' [22]. With a strong awareness of the opaqueness of social structures and the paradox of unintended consequences of human action, Weber still presents sociological knowledge as important for people who want to take a stand on public issues. Despite his central preoccupation with forms of domination in modern society, still he wants to speak of the possibilities for human freedom: 'Weber felt that freedom consists not in realising alleged historical necessities but rather in making deliberate choices between open alternatives. The future is a field for strategy rather than a mere repetition or unfolding of the past. Yet the possibilities for the future are not infinite, nor are they always in the hands of wilful men' [23].

There is a combination of the romantic and the pragmatic in Weber which appealed to Mills. Reference is made to Weber's pragmatic view of the role of ideas. Weber himself expressed it in a memorable way: 'Not ideas, but material and ideal interests directly govern men's conduct. Yet very frequently the "world images" which have been created by "ideas" have, like switchmen, determined the tracks along which action has been pushed by the dynamic of interests' [24]. This allows some autonomy for reason and for the intelligent reflection on public issues where one might play the role of switchman. And those who treated politics as a vocation might still affect the direction in which society moves. This is elegantly expressed in Weber's essay of that title: 'Politics is a strong and slow boring of hard boards. It takes both passion and perspective. Certainly all historical experience confirms the truth — that man would not have attained the possible unless time and again he had reached out for the impossible' [25]. The mix of the romantic and the pragmatic here in Weber could hardly be better illustrated.

Among matters of substance where Weber serves as an intellectual model for Mills we would include the following three elements.

(i) In his methodology Weber wrestles with the central issue of the relationship between the individual and society. On the one side he constructs a sociology of motivation; on the other side his account of social structures recognizes the psychological consequences that they have in the lives of individuals. Society reaches down into the deepest recesses of the individual's existence; but social structures are human constructions and are an arena for conflict and change. Moreover society is susceptible to analysis. This prevents us from treating society as a reification even while we recognize the reality of constraint. It also allows for a continuing role for the application of reason to public life, even if, in part, this means demonstrating the forms of irrationality and unfreedom which may prevail in industrial societies.

(ii) Conceptually, the issue of power pervades Weber's writing. Whether he is referring to personal relations, where one person is able to realize his or her ends over and against the will of another, or of relations between nation states, this is evident. In between these two extremes there are considerations relating to the distribution of power in particular organizations or between one sector of society and another. Weber's typology of social action, of legitimation and forms of domination all revolve round this, together with his continuing interest in the nature of charismatic leadership. The treatment of power does not, of course, simply deal with questions of naked force but with the ways in which obedience to the will of others may be internalized and with the ways in which ideologies may be promulgated as cloaks for material and ideal interests. Insofar as sociology uncovers some of this activity it constitutes a debunking motif. When applied to contemporary affairs this gives it some affinity to the work of Veblen and to the American muckrakers with which, as we have seen, Mills was familiar and sympathetic. Whatever the last word may be on Weber's contribution to the value freedom debate, there is no doubt that in practice his style could be heavily ironic, whether at the pretensions of the Kaiser or the ideological claims of the revolutionary left.

(iii) Weber's analysis of social stratification is of course derivative upon his view of power. Class, status and party are seen as phenomena of the distribution of power. The relationship between these three categories is seen by Weber as being logically and empirically variable. In particular, he resists any form of economic determinism. One can use deterministic models for heuristic purposes but they should never be confused with reality. The distinction between class and status in Weber is also associated with his discussion of 'life chances', as related to questions of property ownership and market situation; and 'life style' as related to status position. Hence there is entailed an interest not only in forces of production and relations of production, but also in patterns of consumption – their distribution and differentiation throughout the social order [26].

All of these considerations come to permeate Mills's own work, strengthened and developed by other intellectual supports no doubt. The linking of 'subjective' and 'objective' in Gerth and Mills's *Character and Social Structure* represents a form of social analysis in the Weberian tradition. Substantively, the analysis of 'high capitalism' and the role of bureaucracy in industrial societies is explicitly Weberian. In *White Collar,* the treatment of status is worked through on Weberian lines. This allows him to look at white collar categories in general and differentiated terms. They are differentiated in terms of occupational positions, organizational hierarchies and life styles. Yet they manifest status anxiety and panic in a competitive system and objectively are relatively powerless. In *The Power Elite* Mills refuses to accept a ruling class model as his point of departure on the grounds that it presumes too much. The relationship between the political, military and economic orders was empirically complex and it did not help to speak about economic factors being determining in the last instance. Nevertheless, the outcome in terms of the concentration of power at the apex of these hierarchies would, Mills thought, be clearly depicted and some of the main directions of influence between one order and another teased out.

Weber's comments on state socialism may also have left their imprint on Mills. Mills was never a member of any political party and certainly never felt the need to serve as an apologist for Stalin. State bureaucracy and the irresponsible use of power by those who directed the state machine in the Soviet Union could also be identified as moral targets in his sociology. Vulgar, unexamined, Marxism was never a likely option for Mills to choose. This helps to contextualize his later involvement with the New Left, born as it was out of a rejection of Stalinism and the crises in socialism brought about by Soviet military interventions in Eastern Europe, especially in Hungary in 1956. Mills's non-aligned socialism was in accord with the socialist humanism of the New Left. For this he was, from time to time, to find himself attacked by the 'true believers' of the old left, as well as by the professional sociologists who stood on an emasculated version of Weber's view of ethical neutrality in the social sciences [27]. This makes for a biography prickly with contention and shot through with irony.

1.3 FROM MARYLAND TO COLUMBIA

Mills taught at the University of Maryland from 1941 to 1945, where he was Assistant Professor of Sociology. He was rejected for war service by the army on medical grounds: he suffered from hyper-tension. He did not therefore have to face the personal question of conscientious objection. In fact he was an opponent of American involvement in the war. This was a very unusual position among American intellectuals. Notable radical social scientists like Barrington Moore Jr. and Herbert Marcuse were active in the State Department. Given Mills's known antipathy to fascism his opposition is the more surprising. It appears to stem from his great suspicion of the Roosevelt administration and the push towards corporate capitalism that he felt it signified notwithstanding its liberal pretensions. The war, he thought, would put the United States onto a permanent war economy footing.

Columbia University was to prove the place where Mills was to stay — from 1945 onwards and it is on that period that we now concentrate. Numbered among the prominent academics in the Sociology Department were Robert Lynd, Robert MacIver, Paul Lazarsfeld and Robert Merton. Columbia also became a base for emigré scholars from Germany. The Frankfurt School in exile had been re-established as the International Institute for Social Research in the mid-1930s. Among that scholarly community were numbered Adorno, Fromm, Horkheimer, Lowenthal, Marcuse, Neumann and Pollock [28].

In Lynd, we might suppose, Mills saw something of a kindred spirit. After all, Robert and Helen Lynd had produced the pioneering Middletown studies. The second volume, particularly, stressed the role of economic power and the gap between formal democracy and the nature of decision making [29]. As such it was the kind of concrete evidence Mills would draw upon in *White Collar* and *The Power Elite*. Certainly he was far more attuned to this than the Yankee City studies of W. Lloyd Warner and his associates, whose treatment of class he regarded as hopelessly muddled [30].

Lynd had also published *Knowledge for What?* In 1939. In a number of ways this anticipated *The Sociological Imagination* written some twenty years later. It was not Mills but Lynd who elsewhere had written:

> Liberal democracy has never dared face the fact that industrial capitalism is an intensely coercive form of organisation of society that cumulatively constrains men and all of their institutions to work the will of the minority who hold and wield economic power; and that this relentless warping of men's lives and forms of association become less and less the results of voluntary decisions by 'bad' or 'good' men and more and more an impersonal web of coercions dictated by the need to keep 'the system' running. [31]

The difference between them was in Lynd's emphasis on the primacy of the economic in explaining power. For this reason Lynd never accepted Mills's use of the power elite concept, since for him the ruling class, with its economic resonances, was the appropriate point of departure.

Ten years after *Knowledge for What?* Lynd wrote an article for *The New Republic* entitled, 'The Science of Inhuman Relations.' In it he attacked Samuel Stouffer's study, *The American Soldier,* on the ground that it provided knowledge about how to control people for purposes not of their own willing. This threatened to make social science an instrument of mass control, rather than the strengthening of democracy that it should be. Given Mills's view about the war, it is not surprising that he incorporated this reference into *The Sociological Imagination* [32].

When Mills went to Columbia, Robert Merton was already well established there. Although the tone and style of their writing is very different, it is really quite remarkable to see how their substantive concerns and interests overlap. Both, in their early years, made significant contributions to the sociology of knowledge and cross-reference each other's work. They were almost the only two American sociologists working in that area in the late 1930s and early 1940s. Merton's essay 'The Sociology of Knowledge' sets up a paradigm for theory in this field [33]. There are very thorough discussions of Marx, Mannheim and Durkheim. On the problem of Marxist causal analysis of the relation between knowledge and society and the use of terms like 'determination', 'correspondence', and 'reflection', Merton follows Mills's Language, Logic and Culture. He also follows through the relevance of audiences or publics for a social theory of knowledge:

> Men of knowledge do not orient themselves exclusively toward the total society, but to special segments of that society with their special demands, criteria of validity, of significant knowledge, of pertinent problems etc. It is through integration of these demands and expectations of particular audiences, which can be effectively located in the social structure, that men of knowledge organise their own work, define their data, seize upon their problems. [34]

Merton's work is permeated with the European tradition every bit as much as Mills's. His essays on bureaucracy are a prime example of his response to Weber, where he develops Weber's idea of the unintended consequences of planned purposive action to the study of large organisations. Moreover, Merton shares with Mills a strong appreciation of the relationship between social structure and personality. This is evident not only in his essays on bureaucracy, but in his famous anomie paradigm and in his extensive discussion of role and reference groups. His interest in the social role of the intellectual is considerable and probably more subtle in its ramifications than Mills's analysis. His essays on the relationship between theory and research are lucidly written. In particular, his discussion of concept formation and refinement together with his comments on the role of serendipity in social research, run parallel to the kinds of concern that were to surface a little later in Mills's *The Sociological Imagination* [35].

Merton, as noted elsewhere, wrote an approving foreword to *Character and Social Structure*. Mills, one suspects, like another radical sociologist, Alvin Gouldner, respected Merton's academic judgements. It is Gouldner, a one-time student of Merton's, who has noted the affinities and complementarities between Merton and Mills. He describes Merton's work on anomie and Mills's on 'social pathology' as liberating. The particular Mills essay he has in mind is 'The Professional Ideology of the Social Pathologists' [36]. This contribution to the sociology of knowledge examines the way in which American sociology in the first half of the twentieth century, neglected the analysis of social structure. Consequently, industrial capitalism was taken as the norm for American society, instead of itself being examined as problematic. Sequences of problem situations are not linked into structures. Such models, Mills argued, smuggle in unexamined values and, insofar as they consider social change, they do so from a perspective of continuous evolutionary change. Anything that deviates from that is defined as 'abnormal', so discontinuity is counted as disorganization, whereas from some radical points of view it might be treated as reorganization.

Both Merton and Mills were keenly aware that to avoid analysing social structures was to give hostages to the status quo. Gouldner observed that both Merton and Mills remained open to Marxist theory. Merton has endorsed this point and cites Gouldner's comment with approval in a recent essay:

> both Merton and Mills kept open an avenue of access to Marxist theory. Indeed both of them had a kind of tacit Marxism. Mills's Marxism was always much more tacit than his own radical position made it seem; while Merton was always much more Marxist than his silences on that question may make it seem ... Merton always knew his Marx and knew thoroughly the nuances of controversy in living Marxist culture. [37]

Columbia also became a centre for mass media research. The essay, 'Studies in Radio and Film Propaganda', written by Merton and Lazarsfeld, reminds us of their collaboration in this field under the auspices of the Bureau for Applied Social Research [38]. Lazarsfeld described Merton's decision to join the Bureau as the most important event in its history [39]. The Columbia situation stimulated Mills's work on the mass media. The extent of this interest will emerge as we proceed. He worked in association with Lazarsfeld at the Bureau. Here we will mention one paper, 'Mass Media and Public Opinion' which had been intended for publication in a Russian language paper but was prohibited by the Soviet authorities [40]. Mills makes a distinction between primary publics and mass publics and expresses concern about the expropriation of information and the possibility of manipulation of the wider public from centralized points of control.

Mills sees a threat to democracy in this trend but is less pessimistic than in his later writings:

> The American public is neither a sandheap of individuals each making up his own mind, nor a regimented mass manipulated by monopolised media of communication. The American public is a complex, informal network of persons and small groups interchanging on all occupational and class levels, opinions and information, and variously exposed to the different types of mass media and their varying contents. There are many influences at work upon these publics and masses and within them, and there are many resistances and counter-forces to these various influences. But today it is still the case that the most effective and immediate context of changing opinion is people talking informally with people. [41]

Much of Mills's later work was a monitoring of this view in the light of tendencies towards a mass society which he detected. The monopolization of the means of communication was, for him, a step in the direction of totalitarianism and therefore strategies of resistance should be located and stimulated. The ability to answer back and access to the means of communication were, for Mills, an important indicator of the health of a democratic society.

While attached to the Bureau, Mills was involved in a range of work, notably his trade union study, *The New Men of Power*, and his immigrant research project published as *Puerto Rican Journey*. A good deal of the material for *White Collar* also came from work accomplished under the auspices of the Bureau. Clearly, Mills became uncomfortable in the Bureau. His strongest statements eventually appeared in *The Sociological Imagination* with an explicit attack on Lazarsfeld who, for his part, was to accuse Mills of advancing 'charlatanism not knowledge' [42]. Before that, however, Mills could be observed taking aim in a 1952 paper, 'Two Styles of Social Science Research [43]. The two styles in question were the molecular and the macroscopic. What he was interested in doing was to argue that, both in formulating research problems and explanations. it was necessary to shuttle between the molecular and the macroscopic. In this way proper attention could be given to questions of concept formation and empirically based indices, whilst anchoring the study in a structural context. In some ways this is not so different from Merton's discussion of theories of the middle range [44]. However, in the process of discussing molecular work, Mills identifies it with the kind of empirical work everyone knew the Bureau was doing. He suggested that such research tended to be at the behest of the client, such as a government department, the army or a business concern:

Accordingly, there is little doubt that the applied focus has tended to lower the intellectual initiative and to heighten the opportunism of the researcher. However, technically free he may be, his initiative and interest are in fact usually subordinate to those of the client whether it be the selling of pulp magazines or the administration of the army's morale. [45]

Mills's overarching point was that even if the one person could not undertake the whole research task, a consciousness of the need to blend these two styles of research would lead to a practical division of labour and produce a sociology that would be relevant to the general public and not just to a privileged client.

The Columbia period coincided with most of Mills's published output. Despite his misgivings about the Bureau, his own debt to it should be recognized. The materials that he was able to gather, the research colleagues he worked with, the funding which made the work possible were all indispensable to the successful completion of *The New Men of Power, Puerto Rican Journey, White Collar* and *The Power Elite*.

From the mid-1950s until 1961 Mills travelled extensively in Europe and Latin America. He visited the Soviet Union, spent time in France and Scandinavia. In 1959, he was a visitor to the London School of Economics. He became increasingly concerned about the two issues which have continued to dominate world politics — the dangers of a thermonuclear war and the relations between rich and poor countries. His books, *The Causes of World War III* and *Listen Yankee: the Revolution in Cuba* were a direct expression of this — a late flowering, perhaps of the American muckraking tradition. The books were widely read in Europe and the United States and provoked much controversy. His death in 1962 occurred some months before the Cuban missile crisis, an event which symbolized very dramatically and dangerously the interconnections between the East—West cold war and the North—South poverty gap.

Since Mills became more and more identified as a radical sociologist during the 1950s — an outspoken critic of American society and foreign policy, as well as of many of his sociological colleagues — something should be said about this and, more especially, his relationship to Marxism.

Mills's longstanding interest in pragmatism and the muckraking tradition gave him a developed interest in the relationship between theory and practice. Was it really possible through the application of knowledge and critical intelligence to re-make the world? Mills's eventual quarrel with American pragmatism was that it had lost its critical edge. Although attempts were made by American writers like Sydney Hook to combine Marxism and pragmatism, in the main the two perspectives were treated in oppositional terms. Dewey, as a notable example, wrote *Why I am not a Communist.* Some of these influences remained with Mills. Moreover his muckraking 'wobbly' sympathies also made him suspicious of big parties, or autocratic leaders who tend to enforce 'correct' lines without proper rational debate. Hence he strongly disliked what he observed of the Communist Party in America and also of the operation of bureaucracy and Stalinism in the Soviet Union.

Yet whatever his dislike of absolutist or monolithic left-wing positions, he was just as critical of those who, in the 1950s proclaimed 'the end of ideology'. The issues surrounding the debate are quite complex and it is not possible in this context to disentangle all the different elements. A good summary of many of the contributions is found in Chaim Waxman's edited selection, *The End of Ideology Debate* [46].

The assertions involved in 'the end of ideology' position ranged from statements about the death of political philosophy, the decline of ideology in the West — associated with the emergence of consensus politics — the undesirability of 'utopian' stances as against 'social engineering' or the 'fine tuning' of political and economic institutions. Among the American writers sympathetic to one or another version of the 'the end of ideology' thesis were Daniel Bell, S. M. Lipset and Edward Shils. All are represented in the Waxman volume. Shils gives an account of the Milan Conference of the Congress of Cultural Freedom, held in 1955, in which many of these issues were aired by philosophers, social scientists and politicians. Also reprinted is Bell's much cited essay, 'The End of Ideology in the West'. Ideology for Bell has strongly negative connotations — as in fascism and Stalinism. Ideologists are 'terrible simplifiers'; 'Ideology makes it unnecessary for people to confront individual issues on their individual merits. One simply turns the ideological vending machine, and out come prepared formulae. And when these beliefs are suffused by apocalyptic fervour, ideas become weapons, and with dreadful results' [47]. Bell goes on to criticize the New Left for being vague about where they want socialism to go (which does not sound like the prepared formulae he was earlier complaining about, not cut and dried enough it would seem). He accuses them of accepting all revolutionary movements without regard for what they concretely signify, or the means they use to achieve their objectives. To go beyond ideology, he claims, must mean to go beyond rhetoric, including the rhetoric of revolution.

Mills was in sympathetic contact with the New Left, especially in Britain. In his 'Letter to the New Left', also reprinted in Waxman, he criticizes those who espouse the 'the end of ideology' thesis. He suggests that for some it signifies a refusal to make any genuine commitment to socialism. Some former socialist intellectuals were burnt-out cases, some were cynically withdrawing from political reflection. The end result was to justify the status quo, which, given the nature of the Cold War and the divide between the rich and poor nations was a complacent and indefensible position. He saw it as a mechanical response to Stalinism. There is, Mills argues, a crucial distinction to be made between celebrating society as a going concern and making space for a critique of society. This critique was to be conducted not in terms of dogmatism, fanaticism, bogus rhetoric or the kind of negative formulations put forward by the end of ideology proponents as characteristic of the New Left. Rather it was to take as its source and inspiration the humanist and secular ideals of Western civilization embodied in the principles of reason, freedom and justice. Why should these ideals be subverted by others? Why should the devil have all the best tunes?

Nor does Mills ignore the charge of utopianism. What he suggests is that utopianism in present circumstances is both desirable and realistic. Such utopianism is a source of strength not weakness. The need for radical change is thereby underscored:

> What needs to be understood, and what needs to be changed, is not first this and then that detail of some institution or policy. If there is to be a politics of the New Left, what needs to be analysed is the *structure* of institutions, the *foundation* of policies. In this sense, both in its criticisms and in its proposals, our work is necessarily structural — and so *for us* just now — utopian. [48]

Mills goes on to point out that theories about the agencies of social change in industrial societies, including Marxist theories need to be re-examined. He is not convinced that the working class will necessarily be the most important agency. Indeed, he moves to a general position where the intelligentsia — the cultural workers, especially the younger generation, will, he thinks, have a crucial role to play. In different ways he sees this applying in the East, West and in the third world.

In the third world the intelligentsia could already be seen to be playing an active part in radical social change. Cuba was for Mills an especially impressive example. In the East and West what Mills looked for was a way in which intellectuals could put their cultural alienation to work, by using the cultural apparatus. Critiques of state socialism and welfare capitalism could be mounted to throw into sharp focus the crackpot realism of the powerful, who treated the preparation for war as normal and necessary. This is what he meant by practising the politics of truth: 'The intellectual ought to be the moral conscience of his society, at least with reference to the value of truth, for in the defining instance, that *is* his politics. And he ought also to be a man absorbed in the attempt to know what is real and what is normal' [49].

Mills does attempt to settle his account with Marxism in the posthumously published book, *The Marxists*. The book itself contains a collection of Marxist writings including Marx, Engels, Lenin, Trotsky. Stalin, Luxemburg, Mao Tse-Tung, Kautsky, Bernstein, Togliatti and Kruschev. The first seven chapters, however, constitute a critical discourse of Marx and Marxism. We will now indicate some of the salient aspects of the text.

First, Marxism is recognized as having made an enormous contribution to the social sciences. Mills chooses to locate Marxism within the social science tradition rather than write of a Marxist social science:

> No-one who does not come to grips with the ideas of marxism can be an adequate social scientist: no one who believes that marxism contains the last word can be one either. Is there any doubt about this after Max Weber, Thorstein Veblen, Karl Mannheim — to mention only three? We do now have ways — better than Marx's alone — of studying and understanding man, society and history, but the work of these three is quite unimaginable without his work. [50]

This remark was directed at both social scientists and Marxists. Mills thought that in the United States there was often a lack of awareness of the contribution of Marxism to social science and that this was a mark of intellectual provincialism. We would suggest that however generally true that may have been, Mills was not a voice in the wilderness in this respect. Attention has already been drawn to Merton's awareness of and use of the Marxist heritage. The case of Talcott Parsons might also be mentioned. His treatment of Marx throughout the corpus of his writings was undoubtedly muted. Yet it is interesting to recall that, in 1948, he took part in a meeting of the American Economic Association convened on the hundredth anniversary of the publication of *The Communist Manifesto*. His paper, Social Classes and Class Conflict in the Light of Recent Sociological Theory, paid generous tribute to the influence of Marxist ideas as a point of departure for modern sociological theory [51]. For example, he concluded that the Marxist view of the importance of class structure has 'in a broad way been vindicated'. Marx and Engels were true social scientists whose work was a 'major stimulus' and who 'formed an indispensable link in the chain of development of social science' [52]

Secondly, Mills outlines how he thinks Marx's work should be used. Here he makes a three-fold distinction between Vulgar Marxism, Sophisticated Marxism and Plain Marxism. Vulgar Marxists are those who operate with and within a closed ideological system, who settle questions by fiat or appeal to authority. This is the fundamentalist, true believer, approach to Marxism. Sophisticated Marxists are those who are wedded to a Marxist model of society and deal with empirical and theoretical problems which arise from examining the world, by saving clauses or conceptual elaborations designed at all costs to save the model. By recognizing that a variety of theories — that is, propositional statements about relations between elements in a model and their causal significance — can be derived from the model, this leads to some elasticity. But, by treating the model as sacrosanct — that is, the inventory of elements considered necessary for orientating analysis — there are outer limits to social analysis beyond which the sophisticated Marxist will not go.

Plain Marxists recognize the great importance of the Marxist model and ways of thinking. Many, though not all, stand outside party allegiances and operate as critical thinkers in relation to Marx as to other social theorists, in the spirit of Marx's own critical work in his own generation:

> in their work, plain marxists have stressed the humanism of marxism, especially of the younger Marx, and the role of the superstructure in history; they have pointed out that to underemphasise the *interplay* of bases and superstructures in the making of history is to transform men into that abstraction for which Marx criticised Feurbach. They have been 'open'

(as opposed to dogmatic) in their interpretations and use of marxism. They have stressed that 'economic determinism' is, after all, a matter of degree, and held that it is so used in Marx's own writings, especially in his historical essays. They have emphasised the volition of men in the making of history − their freedom − in contrast to any determinist laws of history and accordingly the lack of individual responsibility. [53]

Numbered among the Plain Marxists are people as various as William Morris, Antonio Gramsci, Rosa Luxemberg, G. D. H. Cole, Jean-Paul Sartre, E. P. Thompson and Lezlo Kolokowski.

Mills clearly reveals his own sympathy with the Plain Marxists. However, after elaborating an extensive inventory of the constituents of the Marxist model he subjects it to critical scrutiny. The deficiencies in the model, as he sees it, amount to a formidable list: inadequacies in the categories of stratification; ambiguities and inaccuracies about the significance and political consequences arising from changes in the economic base; an erroneous theory of power and of the role of the state. Especially singled out for attack is Marx's view of the role of the working class as an agency of revolutionary change. Class struggle, in the Marxist sense, he concludes, does not prevail in advanced capitalist societies. Since this is so central in Marx's model, much also collapses with the demise of the labour metaphysic. All this leads Mills to state without reservation that Marx's general model of society was inadequate − and the 'laws of the dialectic' are dismissed in an extended footnote as either a mass of platitudes, a way of double-talk, a pretentious obscurantism, or all three [54]. What is left? A method which shows us how to develop critical enquiry. That method takes us 'beyond Marx'. In doing so it breaks the mould of the original Marxist model.

Just as pragmatism lost its way, in Mills's view, by contributing to the liberal rhetoric in the United States, rather than remaining faithful to its activity of applying critical intelligence to social life, so Marxism has succumbed to Vulgar Marxism in the Soviet Union. So it is that liberalism and Marxism, both inheritors of the Enlightenment, have ironically been transformed into instruments of unreason and unfreedom. That is why, in Mills's view, we need to go beyond liberalism and beyond communism. One role for the intellectual is to show why existing liberal and Marxist models are inadequate and what is actually being done in their name underneath the rhetoric. To say that we must go beyond liberalism or beyond Marxism is to hold out the possibility that alternatives to our present world order might still be imagined. Imagination is the beginning of wisdom. Concrete thinking and action still remain to be accomplished. For some this might involve what some of Mills's radical successors were to describe as the long march through the institutions.

By the end of his life Mills's general intellectual perspective could be described as a radical pragmatism provoked by a Marxist humanism. The hope was that intellectuals might be sufficiently aware of the world contexts in which we live that they might, through the use of critical intelligence and the deployment of the politics of truth, help us to inch away from the dangers that threaten the survival of the species and the planet. We can, he thought, choose to avoid our 'fate' and cultural workmen must direct all their energies to that momentous task.

2

The Intellectual Craftsman

2.1 INTELLECTUAL CRAFTSMANSHIP

As a prelude to an exposition of Mills's work we will do two things: first establish what he meant by intellectual craftmanship and secondly draw attention to some stylistic features which characterize his sociological writing.

Mills offers this advice to would-be sociologists:

> Be a good craftsman. Avoid any rigid set of procedures. Above all seek to develop and to use the sociological imagination. Avoid the fetishism of method and technique. Urge the rehabilitation of the unpretentious intellectual craftsman and try to become such a craftsman yourself. Let every man be his own methodologist; let every man be his own theorist: let theory and method again become part of the practice of the craft. [1]

What Mills hoped was that sociologists would take control of their own work and live their scholarship rather than simply live off it. Craftsmen co-ordinate head and hand, knowledge and experience; they follow traditions but also have the capacity to innovate. The individual style of the craftsman's work bears the imprint of his personality. His signature is upon what he produces, as it were, representing an involvement and pride in what is accomplished. Such work may properly be described as a vocation.

Cultural workmen should be discouraged therefore from slavishly following established research procedures or from using received theories in an unreflective way. That is no way to take control of one's own product. Even so, defining and analysing a research problem does not take place in isolation outside the classic tradition of social science into which we enter, so to speak, as apprentices. But if the tradition is to be a living one we must do our own creative work. This is not done in total isolation. There is a need to communicate with other scholars through their written work and sometimes personally. Alongside this there is a need to meet people outside the world of scholarship who may have practical knowledge and experience of the particular problem we are interested in. This is part of what Mills means by the fusion of intellectual and personal life.

Enough has been said to indicate that Mills's call for everyone to be their own theorist and methodologist was not a concession to sloppiness or a prescription for 'abandoning method'. What it entailed was a critical engagement with the received tradition. Indeed, in a conscious send-up of his own preference for plain talk, which nevertheless underlines the significance of the point, he expressed the matter in the following formal terms:

> Problematical situations have to be formulated with due attention to their conceptual and theoretical implications, and also to appropriate paradigms of empirical research and suitable models of verification. These paradigms and models in turn, must be so constructed that they permit further theoretical and conceptual implications to be drawn from their employment. The theoretical and conceptual implications of problematic situations should first be fully explored. To do this requires the social scientist to specify each such implication and consider it in relation to every other one, but also in such a way that it fits the paradigms of empirical reasearch and the models of verification. [2]

That statement harks back to Mills's pragmatism — Dewey surely would have approved of it — and to his early interest in the sociology of knowledge. Clearly the innovative work of the intellectual craftsman is to be understood in the context of the rigorous discipline of reasoning. In the process of stimulating the sociological imagination Mills particularly emphasizes the explicit and systematic attention that should be paid to new possibilities for classifying materials. Of particular interest is his comment on the techniques of cross-classification:

> For the working sociologist, cross-classification is what dia-gramming a sentence is for a diligent grammarian. In many ways cross-classification is the very grammar of the sociological imagination. Like all grammar it must be controlled and not allowed to run away from its purpose'. [3]

As the use of language is governed by many implicit rules, so it is with sociology. By the same token there is a rich diversity of linguistic form and expression and continual possibilities for innovation which the rules make possible and the same principle holds good for socio-logical work.

As Mills describes it the technique of cross-classification can be applied to quantitative or qualitative data. The cross-tabulations of the statistician are of course a standard procedure. Yet to cross-tabulate age data with, say, income data, carries with it conceptual implications and views about possible relationships. However, as a more developed example of the technique of cross-classification, we may consider an example drawn from Mills's paper, 'The contributions of Sociology to the Study of Industrial Relations [4].

Subjective condition of individual	Objective structure of power	
	Participates	Does not participate
Cheerful and willing	1. The unalienated worker	2. Manipulated pseudo-morale
Not cheerful and unwilling	3. Malcontent; the unadjusted worker	4. The alienated worker

The over-riding intention here is to specify some possible relationships between subjective feelings of work satisfaction or dissatisfaction and the structure of power within which work is actually carried out. At the time he was writing the human relations school of industrial socio-logy was pre-eminent in the United States and notably associated with the work of Elton Mayo. Mills argued that this approach was essentially a tool of management because the concern to enhance job satisfaction simply took the existing power structure within and surrounding the industrial enterprise, for granted. In effect therefore only categories

2 and 4 came into the researcher's vision. The object of the human relations exercise essentially could be defined as showing how workers by various therapeutic techniques and group experiments could be moved from the alienated to the manipulated category.

By introducing the question of power several things happen. The limitations of the then conventional paradigm in American industrial sociology are more clearly revealed, together with its ideological underpinning. The introduction of categories 1 and 3 permit new ways of thinking about the position of the industrial worker. Alongside this the possibility of developing an alternative ideology about preferred outcomes is also made available. His own values no doubt led him to look for the kind of social change that would promote a situation where most workers would be located in category 1. Precisely through the application of cross-classifactory techniques new types are formulated which also serve the purpose of criticizing and clarifying old ones. What also follows is that these conceptual innovations crucially affect the way empirical data is handled and interpreted. Hence a critique of the way in which 'objective' indices of job satisfaction or alienation may be mounted if in fact they have only been connected to categories 2 and 4. The significance of the empirical work must be seen in the light of the overall conceptual perspective. The chart in itself does not tell us anything about mechanisms whereby workers move from one category to another, but it does provide us with new ways of thinking about the nature of such changes and therefore is a stimulus to research activity.

The above example may serve to make more general points about cross-classification. First, the innovatory possibilities which the technique embodies suggest that the new concepts might help us to understand reality more closely than the use of the old concepts permitted. In other words, a new perspective coming from the mind of the investigator may correspond more clearly to what is happening in the world. Clearly Mills thought the human relations perspective was inadequate and in some respects erroneous. The implication must be that his own alternative has a greater explanatory power in principle. Now this does challenge the relativistic foundations of Mills's own sociology of knowledge. On the other hand it is consistent with his view that social scientists should seek to provide more adequate definitions of reality.

Secondly, a cross-classificatory frame can exist at different levels of generality. Accordingly, a particular box in the frame may be further subdivided; conversely a frame may be subsumed under a larger perspective. For example, in the above chart it would be possible to develop a typology of the 'unadjusted worker' in a social psychological investigation. On the other hand if a typology of industrial societies was constructed one variation might be the highly bureaucratised corporate capitalist society. One might investigate whether there was an empirical tendency for 'manipulated workers' to predominate in such societies. This kind of linkage is indeed explored in *White Collar* when Mills discusses the morale of 'cheerful robots'. Our attention therefore is drawn not only to the technique of cross-classification but to the interlocking constructions which may link one cross-classificatory system with another. Through these imaginative ways of thinking new analyses can proceed which ultimately will come back to the root problem of how we are to understand the relationship of the individual to society.

Mills's commitment to intellectual craftsmanship as a way of practising the social sciences was a particular expression of a more general ideal. For him the ideal of craftsmanship played something like the part that the abolition of the division of labour played for Marx. The quotation with which we end this section may be regarded as something of a romantic exaggeration so far as serious sociological analysis is concerned, but there is no doubt that it tells us something about Mills's own vocabulary of motivation:

> Human society, in brief, ought to be built around craftsman-
> ship as the central experience of the unalienated human being
> and at the very root of free human development. The most
> fruitful way to define the social problem is to ask how such a
> society can be built. For the highest human ideal is to become
> a good craftsman. [5]

2.2 MILLS'S STYLE AND VOCABULARY

Given Mills's view about the importance of intellectual craftsmanship we may ask whether there are any distinctive marks about his own work. Consider first the opening lines of a number of books which we will be discussing later:

> While older spokesmen are still being heroized, new men are
> accumulating power in America. Inside this country today, the
> labor leaders are the strategic actors; they lead the only
> organizations capable of stopping the main drift towards war
> and slump.
>
> *New Men of Power*

The white collar people slipped quietly into modern society.

White Collar

The powers of ordinary men are circumscribed by the every-day worlds in which they live, yet even in these rounds of job, family and neighbourhood they often seem driven by forces they can either understand nor govern.

Power Elite

Nowadays men often feel that their private lives are a series of traps.

Sociological Imagination

The shock of world events has hit the social sciences harder than many social scientists realise.

Character and Social Structure

These openings attempt to seize the reader's attention. They make a statement, which, whether we agree with it or not, challenges us to read on. Our curiosity is aroused and we are stimulated to continue if only to argue with the writer.

Chapter headings too in Mills's work tend to stand as cryptic headlines. The most developed examples are probably in *The Power Elite* where, among others, we have: 'The Celebrities', 'The Corporate Rich', 'The Warlords', 'The Military Ascendancy', 'The Political Directorate', 'The Higher Immorality'. The slightly unusual juxtaposition of words in a phrase like 'the higher immorality' is a device employed by Mills to stop us in our tracks momentarily. Other examples are: 'organized irresponsibility', 'crackpot realism', 'underdeveloped men in over-developed societies', and 'illiberal practicality'. Such phrases appear at first glance as self-contradictory. Other writers sometimes use the same technique. One thinks for example of Herbert Marcuse's use of the term 'repressive tolerance'. The intention is to illuminate some area of social reality by exploring what such concepts might signify. Somewhat akin to this is the use of two sometimes synonymous terms in a way which brings out a contrast. So Mills refers from time to time to 'men with rationality but without reason'. In this there are sometimes conscious echoes of Mannheim. There are of course more obvious contrast concepts deployed by Mills: 'elites and masses', 'private and public', 'social structure and personal milieu', 'thrust and drift', 'local and metropolitan'. Such concepts can form hinges upon which empirical work and interpretations depend.

Behind many of these formulations is the idea that reality is not always what it appears. So we find this expressed in other ways too.

History happens behind men's backs, Mills claims. We may suffer the consequences of the impersonal drift of history. We may be deceived by a veil of indifference, or by rhetoric (as in liberal rhetoric, the rhetoric of competition) or dazzled by metaphysics (notably military metaphysics and the metaphysic of labour). The muckraking tradition does carry with it the suspicion that official views of the way the world is or should be hide things from us, which in the end is against the public interest.

Writing with special reference to *White Collar*, Richard Gillam makes some observations about Mills's vocabulary which reinforce the point abut the muckraking tradition:

> Mills' obsession with massive size and force became inescapably apparent in its pages. His prose trades in mechanical and military allusion, in metaphors of death and termination: the 'enemy' is 'big', 'giant' or 'mighty' while victims are 'small', 'little', 'weak' or 'dwarfish'. Modern business enterprise, the adversary of democracy is a 'cadre' with a 'military-like' shape. People have become 'robots', 'objects', 'interchangeable parts' or, in an extended description, 'cogs in a business machinery that has routinised and made oppressive an impersonal principle of organisation. . .'. Such central concepts of *White Collar* as the slump—war—boom cycle and the 'garrison state' are also expressive of the violent context that produced them. [6]

The metaphors which occur with great frequency in Mills's writing are engineering and geometrical ones. His early false start on an engineering degree perhaps left its mark. In any event we find him referring to: the higher circles, the triangle of power, pivots (as in pivotal function, moment and event) executive, artistic and literary circles, status mechanisms, the fast moving mechanics of class, the institutional mechanics of our time, the hubs of power, the rims of all wheels of power, the regulation of discontent and the machinery of amusement. Society itself under the weight of these metaphors comes to take on something of the character of a giant machine, out of control and moving in the direction which will bring about its own destruction. Mills is looking for a way of bringing this machine under responsible human control again. To do so is to run the risk of being regarded as a quixotic, ridiculous individual with grandiose ambitions to save the world. Others, however, would define this as heroic and applaud the vision. The intellectual outcast and the cult figure were both experiences which beset Mills as people responded in different ways to his work.

Certainly Mills was fascinated by bigness. At times his descriptions remind one of Ripley's legendary 'Believe it or not' cartoon strip. Two leading examples will suffice. In *White Collar* he describes Macy's store — the Biggest Bazaar in the World: 'Now there are 58 escalators, 29 elevators, and 105 conveyor belts; 26 freight lifts whisk loaded trucks from floor to floor; 75 miles of tubing carry the records of who bought it, who sold it, what it was, how much was paid, when did all this happen' [7]. Mills stands amazed at this emporium which, measured by space or money, is the greatest in the world. The second example is in *The Power Elite* where he describes the Pentagon:

> The most dramatic symbol of the scale and shape of the new military edifice is the Pentagon. This concrete and limestone maze contains the organised brain of the American means of violence. The world's largest office building, the United States Capitol would fit neatly into any one of its five segments. Three football fields would reach only the length of one of its five outer walls. Its seventeen and a half miles of corridor, 40,000-phone switchboards, fifteen miles of pneumatic tubing, 2,100 intercoms, connect with one another and with the world, the 31,000 Penatagonians . . . . [8]

Perhaps in the end it is better to retain the capacity for astonishment at such human constructions at the risk of being labelled naive. Sophisticated people who take such matters for granted can become inured to what it all signifies. Mills continued to ask questions, seeking to understand 'the big picture'. Part of his own personal anxiety one suspects, was because what he came to understand he did not much like and solutions to the problems he analysed were not readily available. There is therefore a mood of pessimism that sets the tone of much of his writing. Writing in the end comes to be defined by Mills as a form of cultural struggle. It is in that light that the more evidently polemical works, *The Causes of World War III* and *Listen Yankee*, should be understood. He sometimes referred to such work as preaching. There are times when he appears to follow the legendary self-advice of the preacher: argument weak here, shout louder. But the style is the man and we will now look more closely at the work as a whole. There are strengths and weaknesses but, we will argue, much that is of continuing value.

2.3 SOCIOLOGY AND PRAGMATISM

Sociology and Pragmatism was published posthumously in 1964, yet it is in fact a revised version of Mills's doctoral disseration and to be understood in the context of his early interest in the sociology of knowledge. The study points to a number of elements in his thought that were to be embellished and utilized in later work. Whatever ultimate reservations Mills had about the American pragmatists he admired them because they emphasized the potential power of human intelligence to control human destiny. The pragmatists did wrestle with the problem of how theory was related to practice. They did see a place for the intellectual in public life. Thought could be applied to human affairs and pragmatism could provide the basis for social criticism. But for such criticism to be effective it had to connect with definite publics and so enter the body politic. In the broadest sense Mills was interested in how this happened in nineteenth-century and early twentieth-century North America. He looked at the role of the emerging higher educational institutions in facilitating this linkage and at some key figures in the pragmatist movement, notably Charles Peirce, William James and John Dewey. Given Mills's known interest in Veblen and G. H. Mead it is surprising that their sympathetic relationship to pragmatism is not fully integrated into the account. This was a deficiency that Mills later acknowledged, but the study as it stands is of great interest, although it is probably one of his least-known works. Yet it does provide a thematic key to much of Mills's sociology.

The early part of *Sociology and Pragmatism* sketches out the changing character of higher education in the USA after the Civil War. Mills traces the process of the general secularization of learning. Behind this was a changing occupational division of labour presented in a shift from an agrarian to an urban society. This shift was accompanied by the spread of utilitarian rationality and the setting up of colleges for practical training in new or expanding middle-class occupations. Finance for schooling moved away from its heavy reliance on religious sources which reflected and extended the trend towards secularisation in the educational sphere. This changing institutional base provides the setting for an intellectual milieu. The changes themselves Mills saw as unplanned and indeed 'going on behind men's backs' — a phrase he frequently used throughout his work and which owes something to Veblen. In this newly industrializing society and its concomitant educational expansion, when new opportunities were opening up for commercial and professional careers, pragmatism as a philosophy emerges. This philosophy, which was a distinctively American development though of course stemming from the European philosophical tradition, was organically connected with a new set of publics.

From a broad-brush discussion of changes in American social

structure and its educational ramifications, Mills goes on to give a fascinating portrait of the members of the Metaphysical Club. This was based at Harvard and was the seed-bed of the pragmatist philosophical movement beginning in the early 1870s. The group constituted, in Mills's view, something approximating a free intelligentsia. They were a varied group of scientists, lawyers, religious humanists and philosophers, rather than a group of academic professional philosophers. Their influence was to be felt far outside the academic sphere. In a memoir on the formation of the group, Peirce had referred to the British philosophical influences of J. S. Mill and Jeremy Bentham as an important point of reference. He also describes the Scottish philosopher Alexander Bain as the grandfather of pragmatism with his definition of belief as that upon which a man is prepared to act. The relation between thought and action was a central preoccupation with the pragmatists although there were considerable variations as to what this entailed among its exponents. In general there was a stress on the usefulness of knowledge and the importance of the experimental method as a means of acquiring it.

One member of the Metaphysical Club who went on to have a distinguished and influential legal career was Oliver Wendell Holmes. In the course of a long life he became Chief Justice of Massachusetts and then Judge in the US Supreme Court, retiring from that position in 1932 at the age of 91. His book on *The Common Law* (1881) emphasized the role of experience rather than logic in the life of the law. Experience here refers to the felt necessities of the time, what is considered to be expedient for the community. It is judges who decide this. Their practice, not their logic, makes law. What Mills finds significant here and is worthy of emphasis, is that Holmes, partly because of his social location in the legal system where he actually exercised great power, explicitly recognizes the role of force and power behind this pragmatist position. If legal decisions are based on considerations of public policy, then not only is the judge powerful but he may also in effect become an agent of dominant groups in society. How decisions are actually made may not, however, be a straightforward matter and Holmes advocates what he terms a competitive theory of truth. The power of truth to get itself accepted is tested in the market as it were. The Constitution is an arena, especially through the legal system where such theories are tested. The Constitution, like life itself, is an experiment. Hence, in the legal sphere pragmatism is associated with liberalism – the competition of ideas in the courts in the context of a view of truth that is related to what is expedient in the public interest. Legal judgements come to embody a continuous series of adjustments which seek to interpret and respond to social changes outside the legal sphere.

The main part of *Sociology and Pragmatism* is taken up with Peirce, James and Dewey. In each case Mills gives biographical accounts followed by extended discussions of their work and its implications. Always he is interested in the way their philosophy is put to work in the world. We will attempt now, in a limited way, to give some appreciation of what he was about.

Peirce was probably the most difficult to write about. His writing is notoriously dense in texture. Mills shows a good knowledge of Peirce's work which he had utilized in early articles in the sociology of knowledge — notably the theory of signs and the way this informs the study of meaning and symbols. But Peirce was not a popularizer like James or Dewey. He was a marginal man in relation to the academic community and in the later part of his life was very isolated. He did not look to a contemporary audience but hoped that some future generation of thinkers would take note of what he had done. This, we now know, has happened.

Peirce's logic was highly technical and much influenced by his early work as a scientist, including work experience of applying science to astronomy, navigation and gravity research. His writings in logic were highly critical of his contemporaries and based upon the laboratory style of enquiry, centring on the processes of conjecture and refutation. He recognized that doubt exists in a world of myriad facts and many different opinions. Despite his later personal isolation one thematic element in Peirce is of the importance of the community of scientists working in the laboratory style of enquiry. This was the way to establish knowledge.

The relationship between scientific knowledge and practice was clearly separated in Peirce. This reflects the acknowledged influence of Kant. In his 1896 essay, 'Science as a guide to conduct', Peirce maintains that since science requires the principle of doubt, an instrumental application of science to the world might well extinguish that necessary doubt. Alternatively, if doubt continues the application is always tentative. Such doubt can paralyse action. Positive science can only rest on experience, that is the experimental mode of enquiry. This mode of enquiry can never provide the kind of certainty, for which those who have to make decisions in the world look. Moreover, the relation between reasoning as a very critical activity for logic and the judgements one is called upon to make in ordinary life was, in Peirce's view, discontinuous. Moral questions were a matter of conscience and this was usually understood to be a matter of following the traditional maxims of one's community. Logic and reason were techniques to be applied in a very limited context. As far as Peirce was concerned this methodological context was insulated from the useful and the practical. To those who only know pragmatism through its popularizers all this is something of a surprise. But can logic and reason be restricted in this way? Mills thought not.

Mills argues that the methods set forth by the pragmatists are not morally, socially or politically neutral. Peirce, he suggests, cannot entirely retreat to a technical preoccupation with the methods of logic. In fact, from his 'outsider' position Peirce was actively dissenting from the prevailing ideologies and practices of the growing capitalist society. He did not want his method to be used in its service, which was itself a moral decision. To do so would be to debase reason: it would support greed and by the same token diminish altruism. Furthermore, given his view of science as a community of enquirers and his realist philosophical position, he was morally opposed to the competitive individualism which marked capitalist society. This opposition was, Mills thought, rooted in Peirce's epistemological position. His head, his heart and his general humanistic perspective were conjoined in a number of ways:

> 1. Methodologically, by making the conditions of successful scientific inquiry exclude selfishness. 2. Ontologically, by making the theory of meaning involve and the purpose of inquiry result in, an increasing rationality of reality itself. Being outside and against the prevailing ends of 'inquiry' he so states inquiry as to avoid these ends and he anchors other humanistic ends in the stuff of reality: concrete reasonableness. 3. If this does not do the job, there is available an ontology of love, which sees the determination and the evolution of the universe as involving sociality and evolutionary love. [9]

For a mere technician Peirce seems to have smuggled in some heavy duty baggage of an ontological kind which Mills, as customs officer, duly apprehends.

Mills's interest in Peirce is partly due to his radically social view of science as a community activity. Knowledge is therefore social and the norms governing the obtaining and evaluation of knowledge are also social. In addition the discussion of the relation between theory and practice in Peirce took place at a level of abstraction which made possible a critique of existing society. Knowledge was not swallowed up in the category of the immediately useful, which in the event makes it an instrument of the dominant groups in society. Even in the more restricted sphere of logic, Peirce's hope that a future audience might find his work and ideas acceptable carries with it the thought that things might change for the better.

James and Dewey were pre-eminently popularizers of the pragmatist movement. Mills makes some instructive contrasts between the two writers and their contribution to liberal thought. James, in the late nineteenth and early twentieth century almost took on the role of an evangelist. His audiences were middle-class groupings inside and outside the university, philosophical clubs, religious societies and the like. In stressing James's key position as a popularizer, Mills suggests that he gives a broad church rather than a sectarian role to pragmatism. Whereas Peirce had been prepared to peg out a place for pragmatism in his careful differentiation between kinds of logic and philosophy, James was in the business of treating pragmatism as a form of mediation. That is to say he wants to identify problems that people feel — intellectual dilemmas about free will and determinism, spiritual dilemmas about the validity of religious experiences or felt conflicts between religion and science, between common sense and philosophy. Always James is at hand to say it is all right, different experiences may each be valid in different contexts. In its particular area of application each mode of experience and style of thinking is seen as useful. The mediation of diversities with all the accompanying pluralist connotations occurs by a process of relativism. Within this 'democratic', 'flexible' friendly philosophy where various truths can be reconciled in a *modus vivendi*, the only real enemy is absolutism. James does not approve of Hegel or any of the great system builders. Mills cites a crucial passage from James's lectures on *Pragmatism*:

> Ought not the existence of the various types of thinking which we have recieved, each so splendid for certain purposes, yet all conflicting still, and neither one of them able to support a claim to absolute veracity, to awaken presumptions favourable to the pragmatistic view that all our theories are *instrumental*, are mental modes of *adaptation* to reality, rather than reveltions or gnostic answers to some divinely instituted world-enigma? ... Certainly the restlessness of the actual thematic situation, the value for some purposes of each thought level, and the inability of either to expel the others decisively, suggest this pragmatistic view. [10]

As a popularizer James came into contact with a variety of audiences facing different dilemmas in a industrializing, increasingly secular society. Through his relativism he is able to address each of them with hope and optimism. He is above all reassuring at the individual level.

The diversity of experience is matched by the diversity of truth. Mills summarizes the significance of James's position in this way:

> the practical, the expedient, the true, the good, the satis-factory, are used as equivalent terms in James at the level of the individual. In this way James' pluralism intersects his pragmatism. For James himself the emphasis is on adjustment and adaptation to the modern world under the general canopy of a general but undogmatic belief in immortality. To antici-pate our conclusion, James represents the 'modern liberal'. His type may be contrasted with Weber's classic account of the Puritan. Generally the attitude toward the present order, on the part of the Puritan was defiance and an attempt to remake it. The modern liberal accepts it with some discrimination and makes an effort to 'better' it. [11]

In general this perspective leads to a piecemeal reformism and a middle-of-the-road approach to social problems. We might suppose that this general orientation would put some distance between James and Mills. At one point Mills does claim that James's individualism was such that he could not think politically or historically about problems. However, in at least three respects there are similarities. First, James was critical of the existing political parties and in American parlance was a 'mugwump' – a political independent. There was a contribution that intellectuals could make, James argued, that was free of political party trappings and which involved the role of education in promoting humanitarian values. Secondly, on humanitarian grounds James typi-cally took the side of the underdog and vigorously attacked American imperialism in the Phillipines and the Spanish-American War. He was a committed supporter of the Anti-Imperialist League. This suggests that he had a little more Puritan defiance in him than Mills gives him credit for. Thirdly, stemming from his belief in personal freedom and his individualism he was against bigness. The sentiments that James expressed on this are in keeping with much that Mills was saying half a century later. He also matches Mills in forthrightness:

> Damn great Empires! including that of the Absolute ... Give me individuals and their spheres of activity ... I am against bigness and greatness in all their forms, and with the invisible, molecular moral forces that work from individual, stealing in through the crannies of the world like so many soft rootlets, or like the capillary oozing of water, and yet rending the hardest monuments of man's pride, if you give them time. The bigger the unit you deal with, the hollower, the more

brutal, the more mendacious is the life displayed. So I am against all big success and big results: and in favour of the eternal forces of truth which always work in the individual. [12]

Mills came to the conclusion in his later work that it was not enough to damn bigness but it was necessary to tame it by making big institutions democratically accountable.

John Dewey was a younger contemporary of Peirce and James. His general philosophical interests were exemplified in substantive concerns with the theory and practice of education. As an education-alist he held influential academic positions in Chicago and Columbia, New York. In a meticulous way Mills traces out Dewey's career: the contexts in which he moved inside and outside the university sphere, the publics to which he addressed himself and the shifts in his interests over a long life. He describes how Dewey's concept of intelligence is rooted in a view of the interaction between the organism and the environment. Human action is seen in biological terms (with explicit credit given to James's *Principles of Psychology*) as a form of adaptation within an evolutionary scheme. Adaptation has a step-by-step character about it and meshes in with Dewey's more generalized reform-ist position and with his view of science as a self-corrective activity. Trial and error activity can be guided by a spirit of enquiry and in this way creative intelligence can be utilized in human practice. Technology, as the handmaiden of creative intelligence, can make human activity more efficient and would appear to be a benevolent element in social evolution in the Dewey paradigm.

With great skill Mills does more than offer an exposition of Dewey's eclectic work. He puts it in the context of the changing social structure of the USA. This allows him not only to comment on the selected publics addressed by Dewey but also to suggest that some changes, particularly the experience of World War I highlighted the difficulties Dewey faced in resolving value questions within his methodological framework.

Using a distinction between mass publics and selected publics (something which recurs in various forms throughout his work) Mills identifies four of the latter for whom Dewey wrote. The four partly overlapping groups were: social and political, technical-philosophical, educational, and a student public. What Dewey conveyed to these groups, albeit with differing emphases, was a liberal pluralist perspective which had its roots in the Jeffersonian ideal of small-scale rural democracy. For him the concept of community was normative not descriptive.

The task of education was to show by example and influence how community could be restored.

Yet in many ways the liberal publics to whom Dewey spoke, despite their intelligence and awareness, had been overwhelmed as far as their basic values were concerned by structural and demographic changes, by the growth of cities and the increasing size of business organizations. They had been pragmatic but it was not enough. Mills is sympathetic to these people who were swept along and submerged by the tide of events:

> Everything the earlier crusading liberals, the Muckrakers, were against was specific: a given town's political corruption, the stock yards, a meat trust, a tobacco trust, a fake advertisement; they were against features of the big industrialisation, of high capitalism. What they gave were Jeffersonian shibboleths: Was government corrupt? Civil service reform. Were there big trusts? Trust-busting. Was there an oligarchy of banks etc.? Wilson's New Freedom – for the small capitalist, including farmers. They experiments. They were specific; they were definitely intelligent. But this was wiped out, sucked into the gyrations: the pattern of objective events, the big structural shifts to high capitalism wiped them out along with their publics and magazines for which they wrote. [13]

The outstanding question that these trends posed was where does it leave democracy. Dewey had argued that without community there can be no democracy. Yet community had been invaded by the impersonal forces of 'the great society'. Dewey placed hope in the educational process, which could restore community through intelligent participation in social processes and the infusion of humanitarian values. In *Freedom and Culture* he attacked Marxists who regarded his piecemeal reformism and reliance on education as a means of restoring America's democratic values as not getting to the root of the problem. Their argument had been that he had not properly understood the role of powerful economic and social forces which would far outweigh any educational changes. Dewey counter-attacked Marxism for what he regarded as its mono-causal amd determinist theory of history, disputing also its claims to scientific status. To concede that would be to allow scope for Marxist praxis. Against this he postulates a liberal-pluralist view of the role of the state, a multi-causal view of social change, and looks for the kind of educational system that can give personal growth and develop habits of mind which secure social change, in the direction of democracy, without introducing disorder.

Mills treats Dewey in a sympathetic way. He shares the nostalgia for the Jeffersonian era. He dislikes bigness and the pecuniary culture generated by high capitalism because he sees these things as anti-democratic in their tendencies. At the same time he shares the Marxist judgement that Dewey does not provide a radical enough analysis of the problems he is confronting. What he does not share is the Marxist solution. This is an early surfacing of the dilemma Mills himself faced throughout much of his work. Essentially he is concerned to trace out the consequences for democracy of living in large industrial societies where there are real conflicts of interest. That is why he thinks that concepts like culture, education and particularly community are used in too bland a way. He sums up the issue very well:

> Different groups of thinkers, classes and institutions have different social values and aims: they want to go to different 'places', they are on the move; or they want to stand 'conservatively' still; they have different work patterns, they encompass and pivot around different systems of objects which their activities are striving to realise and which guide their directions and hence furnish the guiding thread for the emergence of their problems. It is here that 'problems' arise and obviously they involve deep problems of value. Dewey's theory of value is not capable of really handling such situations. The concept of the problem aids in this process of masking. [14]

This is the point of departure for Mills as far as his own sociology is concerned. He shares in the heritage of pragmatism whilst denying the adequacy of its individualistic and somewhat class-restricted solutions. Pragmatism was an energetic expression of middle-class ideology but it was no base upon which to construct a democratic community of publics. Whether such a task could ever be accomplished, given the massive structural transformations that had taken place, was highly uncertain. Even to explore the possibility, however, meant taking seriously problems of power in industrial society rather then disguising the matter by using spongy, harmonistic concepts that did not accord with reality. We will now go on to consider how Mills seeks to do this in his studies of contemporary America.

2.4 'CHARACTER AND SOCIAL STRUCTURE'

Character and Social Structure was co-authored with Hans Gerth, Mills's former teacher at Wisconsin, whose general influence on Mills we have already discussed. It was a genuinely shared venture. Subtitled 'The Psychology of Social Institutions', the book was unusual at the time it was written in that it developed an approach to social psychology which embraced a wide comparative and historical perspective. Today it is still unusual, not least in its attempt to integrate disciplines to promote the analysis of social structures. Given its systematic presentation, the book is commendably clear in its main lines of exposition. In an enthusiastic Foreword Robert Merton says that it gives the reader 'a sense of the intellectual excitement that comes from using the trained imagination to study the psychological meaning of social structures' [15]. Since the book was published some thirty years ago the text as a teaching resource is necessarily dated, but the analysis and style of presentation is still worth considering.

Perhaps the simplest point of departure is to reproduce the model on character and social structure which served as an organizing device for the book [16], see Fig. 1.

Each of the elements in the model is carefully identified and defined. This is a prelude to a more developed exposition, followed by an examination of possible linkages between the elements. Only after that are some of the big questions about the nature of social change, with particular reference to modern societies, taken up. For convenience we will enumerate as succinctly as possible the definitions employed.

1. Organism. The biological and physiological mechanisms of the individual human being.

2. Psychic structure. The integration of feeling, sensation and impulses which are anchored in the organism.

3. Person. The human being as a player of roles, which involves reference to emotions, perceptions and purposes. The behaviour of the person is to be understood in terms of motives rather than in physiological terms of stimulus and response.

4. Character structure. The relatively stabilized integration of the organism's psychic structure linked with the social role of the person. This is the most inclusive term for the individual as a whole entity.

5. Role. This is an analytical term which serves as the major link between character and social structure. Given its key position in the model some further elaboration may be helpful. Gerth and Mills write:

By choosing social role as a major concept we are able to reconstruct the inner experience of the person as well as the institutions which make up an historical social structure. For man as a person ... is composed of the specific roles which he enacts and of the effects of enacting these roles upon himself. And society as a *social structure* is composed of roles as segments variously combined in its total circle of institutions. The organisation of roles is important in building up a particular social structure; it also has psychological implications for the persons who act out the social structure. [17]

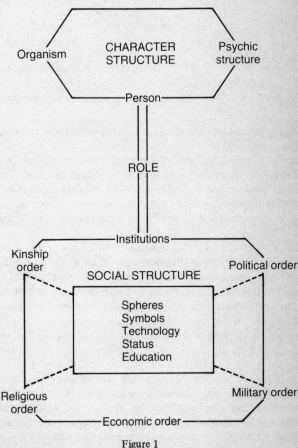

Figure 1

6. Institution. An organization of roles one or more of which is understood to serve the maintenance of the total set of roles.

7. Institutional order. All these institutions within a social structure which have similar consequences and ends or which serve similar objective functions. Political, military, economic, religious and kinship orders are illustrated in the model. How far they are autonomous in particular societies is a matter for investigation.

8. Spheres. Aspects of social conduct which characterize all institutional orders. Five aspects are differentiated:

    a. Symbol sphere. Visual or acoustic signs, expressed for example in ceremonial, language, emblems, music, art, which help us to understand the meaning of human conduct.

    b. Technology. The implementation of conduct with tools, apparatus, machines and instruments and the techniques deployed in the activity.

    c. Status. The agencies and means of distributing prestige or honour among members of the social structure.

    d. Education. Activities concerned with the transmission of skills and values.

9. Social structures. The totality of institutional orders and spheres.

Whatever reservations one might have, this model does represent a conscious and systematic attempt to link together macro and micro considerations of social analysis and to integrate sociology and psychology in a fruitful way. As the model is put to work there are a number of things about it that prove to be instructive. We will touch upon them briefly.

Gerth and Mills in their discussion of character structure are particularly illuminating on the part played by gesture and language in forming and modifying self-images, images of others and of the world. Personal reality and social reality are seen as social constructions. Our experience of these realities is mediated — received, interpreted and re-interpreted — through signs and symbols.

Gestures are seen as being socially and historically determined and as having a grammar of their own, whether or not people are aware of it. So there are vocabularies of gestures and indeed of feelings. The vocabularies are used in everyday life but in addition groups such as poets or novelists may extend or re-interpret them for us. The possibility of correctly interpreting the meaning of gestural and feeling vocabularies is enhanced insofar as certain responses become standardized and expectations are built into recurring situations — shopping, meeting a friend, going to church, playing football or whatever.

Language is given a central place in the whole exposition of *Character and Social Structure*. Perception itself is seen as being organized in terms of symbols and as being influenced by our vocabularies. Elaborating on G. H. Mead's concept of the significant symbol, that is a symbol which means the same thing to different people, the idea of a community of discourse is elaborated. The prime function of language is to be a system of signs which co-ordinates conduct. Attention is thereby drawn to the social context of language use without which meanings cannot be understood. This leads us in the direction of thinking about speech communities, the fruitfulness of which has been more recently evidenced in the work of Dell Hymes among others [18]. Like Hymes, Gerth and Mills take note of anthropological work, notably that of Malinowski. But the general orientation is derived from pragmatism. In addition to Mead's *Mind, Self and Society*, C. W. Morris's *Foundations of the Theory of Signs* and John Dewey's *Experience and Nature* are approvingly referenced.

The importance of language and symbols for Gerth and Mills is nowhere more clearly stated than in their discussion of the sociology of motivation. How and why does human conduct take a particular direction? 'It is clear,' they write, 'that when we speak of understandable motives or intentions, we must pay attention to the social functions of language in interpersonal conduct; we can speak of understanding something only if it is meaningful, and language, a social acquisition and a personal performance, is the prime carrier of meaning. Even dreams have to be deciphered or interpreted as a language of "unconscious impulses" ' [19]. This contention leads Gerth and Mills directly on to consider vocabularies of motive. The reasons we give for our past, present or intended future actions are part of our social conduct. They may seek to justify the past, sustain the present or endorse the future by reference to a vocabulary of motives judged to be acceptable in particular social contexts. Part of the purpose is to convince or persuade others of the appropriateness of our behaviour, or even motivate them to behave in a similar way. There will commonly be a moral element in the vocabulary emphasizing the rightness or wrongness of particular forms of conduct. Although some vocabularies of motives are internalized during childhood, new roles in new social contexts require new vocabularies at later stages in our lives. Experience is reflected upon and conduct is steered through new situations with varying degrees of skill and success. Socialization is not fixed in childhood, therefore, but is a continuing process.

Gerth and Mills suggest that as institutional contexts undergo historical change (for example, the movement from *laisser-faire* to monopoly capitalism) vocabularies of motive change. Vocabularies of motive can become outmoded, they may need to be discarded, modified or accommodated to make room for competing vocabularies. A broad contrast may be made between societies in which a single vocabulary of motives may be used by a person in all of his or her roles and are unquestioned and therefore acceptable to the self and to others, and a society in which a range of vocabularies exist for different situations and in which conflicts, confusions and self-questionings may exist.

This contrast is another way of approaching the community/ association distinction — the small, intimate community set against the large-scale, impersonal industrial society. In a significant passage Gerth and Mills observe:

> Back of the motive-mongering and self-doubts of persons as to their own motives is the fact that in modern life there is often no stable or unquestioned vocabulary of motives available. And back of this is the fact that the institutional arrangements of roles demand that we rapidly give up and take on roles and along with them their socially appropriate motives. Back of these 'mixed motives' and 'motivational conflicts' there is going on a competition of varying institutional patterns and of their respective vocabularies of motives. Shifting and borderline situations, having no stable vocabularies of motive, may contain several alternative sets of motives originally belonging to different systems of roles. [20]

Language, then, interprets social structures to us and when language itself is studied as a set of available symbols it may tell us something about the nature of particular social structures. This perspective goes on to inform Gerth and Mills's discussion of symbol spheres. There they draw attention to the interplay between justifying symbols of social order, institutional authority and role-enacting persons. The kinds of empirical questions which may be asked are: what kind of conduct or institution does this or that symbol motivate or guarantee? In what institutional orders are given symbols to be found and what is their precise function? These questions, as we can see, are in the pragmatic mould and move us away from postulating a 'common value system'. A unified symbol sphere is not a necessary feature of social integration. Society is an arena in which a struggle to use symbols as a means of legitimizing the social order take place. The arena may sometimes be dominated by master symbols which serve to legitimate the social order. Sometimes there may be more fluid competition between the symbols.

If language is so important then it is but a short step to recognize the strategic place of mass communications in modern society, since those in charge of such media are able to select, associate, manipulate and diffuse symbols. This could, hypothetically, make possible the creation of a unified symbol sphere which does not necessarily reflect a harmonious institutional base. This comes close to saying that attempts may be made to create false consciousness. Who is deceiving whom may not always be clear: 'When there are deep antagonisms in the institutional structure, men seeking to transform power into authority may grasp all the more compulsively for the channels of mass communication, but their monopolisation of these media, does not necessarily mean that the symbols they diffuse will be master symbols' [21]. This concern with the role of the mass media in modern society is something which recurs throughout Mills's writing.

If we turn now more explicitly to the treatment of social structure in Gerth and Mills, we discover a systematic mapping of an approach which is intended to go beyond the descriptive level. Suggestions are made about how comparative studies might be organized and how causal imputations might be made. Leaving on one side the detailed discussion of particular institutional orders (which is in fact undertaken in *Character and Social Structure*) the key to their approach is summarized in the following Fig. 2 [22].

INSTITUTIONAL ORDERS					SPHERES
Political	1				Education
Economic	6	2			Status
Military	7	10	3		Symbols
Religious	8	11	13	4	Technology
Kinship	9	12	14	15	5
	Political	Economic	Military	Religious	Kinship

Fig. 2

The first task in the procedure is to look at the categories 1–5, that is to examine the range and characteristics of each institutional order together with the part played by education, status, symbols and technology in each order. The categories 6–15 indicate possible ramifications of one institutional order upon another. Essentially the idea is that one institutional order may be able to use one or all of the other orders for ends which are relevant to its own order. This does not have to be one-way traffic. But to trace out the pattern of ramifications in a society is to discover the relative power of each institutional order. Insofar as the warp of one institutional order may be the woof of another, we can see that we are dealing with a potentially complex means—end schema. This leads directly on to the suggestion that when we consider how social structures are integrated four analytic types may be differentiated. Any actual society would be unlikely to conform precisely to any one type and empirically integration of whatever type may be tighter or looser when we compare different societies. What the model does is to suggest important guide lines for theoretically informed research. The four analytical types are:

1. Correspondence. Here the social structure is unified by the working out in its several institutional orders of a common structural principle. One example would be liberal capitalist societies such as the United States in the nineteenth century, in which diverse institutional orders unite around the integrative principle of competition.

2. Coincidence. Different structural principles or developments in various orders result in their combined effects producing the same, often unforeseen, outcome of unity for the whole social structure. This is along the lines of Weber's discussion of 'elective affinities' and indeed the relation between Puritanism and modern capitalism is offered as an illuminating instance. It is not suggested that a society could be 'explained' solely by reference to this structural principle.

3. Co-ordination. One or more institutional orders becomes ascendant over other orders thereby directing and regulating them. The one-party totalitarian state as in Nazi Germany serves as an example.

4. Convergence. Two or more institutional orders coincide to the point of fusion. For example in frontier societies the farmer may be the military agent, whose family dwelling place also becomes a military outpost.

By setting out these structural principles of integration Gerth and Mills are pointing to the diversity of ways in which societies may more or less cohere. Moreover, they are advocating an approach which goes far beyond common sense. This is the significance of a distinction, used here and elsewhere in Mills's work, between milieu and structure. Milieu refers to the social settings in which we experience everyday life – the neighbourhood, the work place, the leisure scene. But to understand why over a period of time our experience of daily life can change we have to go below the surface to examine structures. It is in this sense that structural sociology is seen as parallel to depth psychology. Observable changes in milieus are seen as being caused by structural changes in institutional orders. These are not so immediately accessible to direct observation but that is where the social scientist has to direct attention.

What are the implications of this for social theory? Gerth and Mills wish to steer between what they term principled monistic theories and principled dogmatic pluralism. The first is reductionist and determinist as in Vulgar Marxism. Here, with echoes of Weber they clearly state: 'The construction of all human history in accordance with Marx's historical materialism is apt to block open-minded inquiry, for it reduces selected aspects and phases of social history to a series of selected illustrations in proof of the alleged sovereignty of the economic order' [23]. The second approach aims at an *a priori* exhaustiveness, listing all possible causes of historical events and social changes. The worry is that by trying to explain everything such an approach explains nothing. Gerth and Mills argue, again on Weberian lines, that one should search for theories of adequate causation, examining specific historical sequences. The investigator will look for 'those causes which according to experience and the conventional standards of scientific evidence satisfy our curiosity' [24]. Although this point is made programmatically it is fair to add that the kind of procedures they have in mind is exemplified in Weber's essay, 'The Social Causes of the Decay of Ancient Civilisation', on the disintegration of the Roman Empire [25]. This naturally reminds us that social structures exist in history and studies of structural unity can only be identified in the context of social change. This unity may be of differing kinds and its stability and future cannot be assumed. What the Gerth and Mills model does is to provide us with a way of examining the collapse of social orders as well as their integration.

It would be a mistake to think of *Character and Social Structure* as a formal treatise disconnected from Mills's substantive sociological work. Clearly, as we have shown, a great deal of attention is given to conceptual formulations and to ways of analysing the relationship between character structure and social structure. In doing so a radically social view of the individual in his or her social context is propounded. The complex concept of social structure, together with discussion of the mechanisms by which it is articulated, is elaborated in a non-reified way. Despite their 'objective' character, social structures remain human constructions. In this respect a good deal of the ground covered in Berger and Luckman's *The Social Construction of Reality* a decade and a half later had already been well tilled. This point can be extended to note the somewhat similar treatments of social role and language in the two books.

Yet Gerth and Mills see their work as providing tools for reflecting upon and interpreting some of the major transformations that have taken place in modern societies. This is chiefly considered in the last chapter of the book entitled, Master Trends. The central emphasis is on the relevance of the structural principle of co-ordination as applied to the political, military and economic orders in both the USA and the USSR. The power elite thesis, seen in the context of a polarization of the great powers in cold war, is read off from this. In the West the process of bureaucratization accompanied by the parallel growth of corporate capitalism, has meant that liberalism, with its emphasis on individual freedom and free competition, has become undermined. It only exists as political rhetoric. This brings with it the risk that liberal democratic countries may turn in a totalitarian direction: 'Totalitarianism is an imperialist response to the impasse of corporate capitalism. It is a twentieth-century response, occurring in a time when scarcity consciousness predominates and when to many liberal ideologies seem hollow ... Only the complacent and the uninformed can feel assured of liberal and democratic developments in the world today' [26]. This possible lurch towards fascism is matched, as it were, against the totalitarianism of Stalinist Russia.

The overall picture drawn is of two power blocs engaged in an arms race and at the same time competing for hegemony over the under-developed societies. Capitalism and Communism are both available as alternative models for under-developed societies. At the same time Europe is the continent which for strategic, economic and ideological reasons is seen as the focus of the contest between the two great powers.

One can easily see how the reference to the USA as a formal democracy threatened by fascism and the coupling of this with a reference to its imperialist activities would not be an altogether welcome observation in that country. However, from Gerth and Mills's standpoint, not to pursue their analysis would be a betrayal of the role of the intellectual. When the stakes are high the use of reason in the study of society is at a premium:

The nature of key national decisions ... involves long-range perspectives and targets and extended and complex means—ends schemas. These decisions are of global scope and they cross institutional orders into which they ramify and which implement them. There is about such institutional mechanics of our time an unheard of 'momentum' and the decisions accordingly are weighty and grave and often frightful. They affect no less the future of mankind. [27]

Yet in the end the conclusion is not one which supports a version of inevitable drift into war or unfreedom. The possibility that collective movements and forms of organization might emerge to combat this is left on the agenda. Critical reflection upon the experienced situation and an understanding of its structural sources might lead to alternative routes of survival. In this way the pragmatism of Gerth and Mills is carried forward into a global and collective context and distanced from purely individualistic expressions.

2.5 'THE NEW MEN OF POWER'

In this and the next two sections we will concentrate on the three studies which Mills wrote on aspects of power in American society: *The New Men of Power, White Collar* and *The Power Elite*.

The New Men of Power was the first of Mills's books to be published, leaving on one side the Gerth and Mills edited selection of Weber's writings. Formally it is identified as the third report of a research project on the characteristics of American labour leaders which began in 1941. The work is very much a team project and was completed at the time Mills was director of the Labour Research Division of the Bureau of Applied Social Research at Columbia. Only Helen Schneider is listed as a co-author, but one is entitled to wonder, given the extent of help acknowledged in the footnotes, whether others also ought to have been similarly listed. This may tell us something about the character of research bureaux, against which Mills later rebelled. On at least one occasion Mills was on the receiving end of a similar practice. Paul Lazarsfeld's article 'Audience Research in the Movie Field', published in the *American Academy of Political and Social Science* in 1947, footnotes Mills who had prepared the text on which the paper was based. It is difficult to justify.

The dislike of hierarchy and concentrated power sits a little uncomfortably in Mills's work, here and elsewhere, with the conviction that strategic actors in powerful organizations should act responsibly. This conflict between the romantic and the pragmatist is evident at the outset of *The New Men of Power*. In the frontispiece of the book is an extract from a 1947 interview with an unknown worker from Nevada, which reads like a poem:

When the boatload of wobblies came
Up to Everett, the sheriff says
Don't you come no further
Who the hell's your leader anyhow?
   Who's your leader?
And them wobblies yelled right back —
We ain't got no leader
   We're all leaders
And they kept right on comin'.

But if Mills's heart is with the wobblies his thesis is not in praise of anarchy. Rather it is that labour leaders in post-war America lead the only organizations capable of stopping the main drift towards war and slump. The book proceeds to build up a statistical picture of these leaders, to examine the publics which constrain and condition their behaviour, why the main drift is as it is and what is required for the drift to be stopped. He wants to use statistics in order to guard against the anecdotal, but he does not want the statistical detail to filter out the larger issues. His aim is to write a social science report which is politically relevant.

What are labour leaders like? In Mills's view this has to be answered in relation to an understanding of union organization and the nature of the wider society. Union organization, however, is not one-dimensional. Unions can be likened to armies, democratic town meetings, political machines, business enterprises and pressure groups. These analogies may be more or less true in different phases or periods of a union's activity and to some extent may co-exist. Union leaders can be expected to reflect these differing and sometimes competing aspects in the performance of their role. The role contains elements of paradox and ambivalence:

Yet even as the labor leader rebels, he holds back rebellion. He organizes discontent and then sits on it, exploiting it in order to maintain a continuous organization: the labor leader is a manager of discontent. He makes regular what might otherwise be disruptive, both within the industrial routine and within the union which he seeks to establish and maintain. During wars, he may hold down wildcat strikes: during up-swings of the economic cycle, he may encourage sit-down possession of private property. In the slump—war boom of American society, the labor union is a regulator of disgruntle-ment and ebullience, and the labor leader, an agent in the institutional channelling of animosity. [28]

An awareness of these possibilities and the sometimes conflicting elements in the role of the union leader serves to shape and inform the study. In less flexible research hands we might have been left with a specimen of the abstracted empiricism that Mills was to lambast so effectively in *The Sociological Imagination*. The survey was a cross-sectional study of labour leaders sent out in 1946. The postal question-naire was directed at an extensive sample at national, state and city levels to unions affilitated to the American Federation of Labor (AFL) and the Congress of Industrial Unions (CIO) plus a small sample of non-affiliated independent unions. The response rate for the main sample was 40% — consisting of 410 usuable returns. This is quite good for a postal questionnaire but despite a long technical footnote we are still unsure about the significance of the missing 60%. Unfortunately a copy of the questionnaire is not included in the monograph and we are not even told how many questions were asked.

The postal questionnaire is a rather blunt research instrument and it is better at eliciting limited factual statements than reliable attitudinal statements. In the main this questionnaire does seem to have been mainly concerned with factual data. The tables in the book are constructed using the AFL and the CIO as two separate samples and set against factors such as age, education, place of birth (in or outside the USA) job history, union career, father's occupation and country of origin.

Findings such as the following are reported: the successful labour leader enters the union world early and stays late. The AFL leader tends to be older than the CIO leader and not so well educated in formal terms. The AFL is a gerontocracy where there is a tension experienced between the older leaders who have fewer educational qualifications than the younger men further down the hierarchy. The CIO is a professional bureaucracy where age and education are more in line and are reflected in the organizational structure. Only one in ten of the labour leaders were born outside the United States. All labour leaders are drawn predominantly from labour's own ranks: their fathers were wage earners and most of them held jobs in the trade or industry in which they were later to operate as union officials.

Such findings, a snapshot of labour leaders at a particular moment in time, are of interest and they are of course treated more extensively in the tables and commentary. If that were all, however, *The New Men of Power* would be little more than an out of date study. There are quite other reasons for reading it.

First, there is a shrewd account of the publics who have opinions of trade unions and their leaders and which provide a context for interpreting the actions of union officials. Apart from the leaders' own constituents in the organizations which keep them in office or remove them, Mills distinguishes between the small circle of politically alert publics and the great American public of politically passive people, the mass public. The relationship between active and passive publics is a theme which is repeated in Mills's work and the treatment of the matter in *The New Men of Power* is particularly instructive.

The political publics are groups who formulate political principles and ideas. Within these general political orientations are contained images of the role of trade unions and the labour movement. Such images and accompanying views as to what constitutes appropriate policy on union-management relations provide a basis for classifying political publics as left, right or centre. Mills defines six such publics: the far left, the independent left, the liberal centre, the communists, the practical right and the sophisticated conservatives. This requires some elaboration since this differentiation provides the framework for Mills's general argument.

The far left is defined as the Leninist left represented primarily by the two Trotskyist parties. 'The members of this public operate on what is probably the most systematized view of political reality now available. Indeed, it is so well worked out that, for most occasions, people who believe but are not very intelligent can formulate an attitude on any given issue. In this sense, the far left supports its adherents with an almost popish set of ideas' [29]. In general they hold that labour leaders are not radical enough and are holding back working class action to smash capitalism. The main hope for industrial and political transformation lies with the rank and file who have the potential to develop revolutionary consciousness, set up an independent labour party and establish workers' control.

The independent left is not so coherent and organised. They are mostly composed of upper class and professional people, with a strong intellectual component. They do not have the far left's faith and typically consitute discouraged socialists who are prone to a sense of political helplessness. Broadly Mills identifies his own position with this public, which underlines the dilemma he faces in the conclusion of *The New Men of Power*, namely, what is to be done? 'To them unions seem one more bureaucratic net ensnaring the people, part of the whole alien and undemocratic apparatus of control. All the bureaucratic elite, in labor as in business and government, are against the rank and file: they are trying to manage it, and it is immoral that men should be the object of management and manipulation. He is the root, and he is being choked' [30]. There is vague talk around anarchism and syndicalism, with thoughts of the decentralization of control but it is not clearly formulated and the trade union remains for them a formidable apparatus whose function they cannot re-define politically: 'With them, political alertness is becoming a contemplative state rather than a spring of action: they are frequently overwhelmed by visions, but they have no organized will' [31].

The liberal centre is portrayed as a very loose collectivity which includes the New Deal type businessman, an anti-monopoly stance and some populist elements in its politics. In general the trade union status quo is supported and labour leaders who maintain their unions as economic interest groups are applauded for knowing what they are about. Despite the indignation and excitement which the liberal centre may generate in the causes it espouses, Mills defines it all as short-run practicality. It amounts to very little and is often defined by the left as petit-bourgeois screaming. We have met this group already in *Sociology and Pragmatism*.

What about the Communists? This is the only public with a single party as a basis for cohesion, whose core follows the Moscow line. This meant, for example, that before World War II the Communists opposed management and the government in its union policies, but when Russia entered the war the party encouraged the disciplining of the work force in prosecuting the war effort. Mills speaks disparagingly of 'the wondrous party line' but estimates that the Communists were the most important minor party in the union world. He identifies them as Stalinists and appears to share the view of left critics who see them as simply responding to the pressures of the ruling group in the Kremlin. They talk the language of democracy but they do not practise it and are an impediment to the formation of the labour party in the USA.

In referring to the political right Mills distinguishes between the practical right and the sophisticated conservatives. The practical right is seen as an extensive and well-organized segment of the Republican party, standing for the benevolence of unfettered competition. They are anti-union and their politics are basically a means to obtain their economic ends, as instanced in the placing of the Taft—Hartley labour legislation on the statute book. Making money out of business and finding ways of clipping the wings of obstructive labour leaders and radicals is central to their position:

Their ideas are a hodge-podge of anything they can use to throw at the enemy. They do not at the present time have any real ideas about preventing war or stopping the drift to another depression, the condition of the foreign world is improbable nonsense to them, and the economic cycle a great bafflement invented by the theoreticians of the New Deal. [32].

The sophisticated conservatives are much more politically aware than the practical right. They come primarily from the trade association world: 'They tie in solidly with the industry — armed forces — State Department axis and move personally as well as politically within those circles' [33]. Here we have an early reference to what Mills later came to characterize as the power elite. For this group the trade unions exist not to be confronted but to be manipulated. Co-operation can be bought and that is preferable to conflict and of course to socialism. Just as the far left sees the labour leader as split from the rank and file and betraying the interests of the working class, so the sophisticated conservative sees him as the vehicle through which rank and file discontent can be controlled. However, it is the global-political aims of the sophisticated conservatives that ultimately concern Mills. Whereas he believes the thrust of the practical right will lead to slump, the programme of the sophisticated conservatives is to make the world profitable for the USA's business interests. This involves policies of loans to foreign countries, partly to re-establish the international capitalist system after the ravages of war, and partly to try and stop the establishment of left-wing governments, for example in Latin America. Intrinsic to this programme also, Mills claims, is the establishment of a war economy as a long-term activity, as a means of avoiding slump or recovering from it.

In a phrase reminiscent of Veblen, Mills argues that history is going on behnid men's backs and that the main drift in the American political economy is that which is being quietly planned and orchestrated by the sophisticated conservatives. This is perhaps the closest Mills gets to in his writings to a conspiratorial view of history.

Meanwhile the mass public is not aware of these things. What they receive, however, through the mass media is an anti-labour point of view. 'By their omissions and in their whole manner of dramatizing the American scene, particularly their heavy accent upon individual effort and individual ends, the mass media are biased against the labor world' [34]. Even so, as he reports, between 1935 and 1945 the percentage of wage and salary workers joining a trade union had risen from 9.4% to 34.4%. What the general public is perhaps most aware of, Mills thinks, is the noise of battle between the liberal centre, where most labour leaders are located, and the anti-union hostility of the practical conservatives.

What is not so obvious is that the trade unions and the labour leaders, in their defence against the practical right, are driven into alliance with the sophisticated conservatives without realizing the political implications of their actions. The general public, in its vague desire for greater co-operation between business and labour is even less aware of where the main drift is taking their society. At its worst, the forces released by the New Deal with a great amount of liberal rhetoric could result in a new corporate state in which social welfare was more and more subordinated to warfare, in preparation or in practice.

In his stated aim to be politically relevant Mills sees his task as firstly, identifying the main drift, secondly, warning against its dangers, and thirdly, indicating alternative possibilities. This leads him to pose the political question in this way: can the democratic elements of the left triumph against monopoly capitalism as well as against the undemocratic forms of left-wing politics? Can this 'dream' be turned into a programme which could halt and reverse the main drift?

> Classic socialism shares its master purpose with classic democracy. The difference between Thomas Jefferson and Karl Marx is half a century of technological change, during which industry replaced agriculture, the large-scale factory replaced the individual workshop, the dependent wage and salary worker replaced the individual proprietor. Left movements have been a series of desperate attempts to uphold the simple values of classic democracy under conditions of giant technology, monopoly capitalism, and the behemoth state — in short, under conditions of modern life. [35]

In the alternative programme which Mills sketches out there are three interdependent elements: shop-floor democracy, economic planning and the formation of a labour party. The first of these, on inspection, turns out to be an endorsement of G. D. H. Cole's approach to workers' control over the social process of work. This encroaching control against the power of employer and state would require a vast extension of union membership and a dimunition of inter-union rivalries if the solidarity of labour were to be realized. But democracy at the workshop through the instrumentality of the union as a political community is treated as the basis for a social reorganization leading to a more democratic society.

The economic programme is again derivative from Cole. Questions of production, prices, wages and profits would be continuously reviewed industry by industry. But merely to nationalize the means of production and distribution would lead to control from above, unless the industry itself was democratized in concrete organizational terms. Otherwise one form of bureaucratic domination is exchanged for another.

Mills not only has in mind the bureaucracy of the Soviet Union but also the case of Britain where nationalization could be interpreted as a device to shift the burden of profitless industries from the capitalists to the taxpayers. The economic programme would also include measures of income redistribution in favour of working people and appropriate tax reforms.

Without effective political power, however, the workshop democracy and the economic plans would not succeed. Since the sophisticated conservatives are able to use the existing political apparatus to move things in their direction the trade union movement needs to create its own political party and not remain entangled with the two major parties. The conclusion of the matter for Mills is this:

> To have peace and not war, the drift toward a war economy, as facilitated by the moves and demands of the sophisticated conservatives, must be stopped; to have peace without slump, the tactics and policies of the practical right must be overcome. The political and economic power of both must be broken. The power of these giants of main drift is both economically and politically anchored; both unions and an independent labor party are needed to struggle effectivel. [36]

In the end, and not surprisingly, Mills was very pessimistic about the outcome. Not only were the architects of the main drift very firmly entrenched, though not entirely visible to public view, but the intellectual left was very divided and its most democratic elements were the least organized. Moreover, he had little confidence that trade union leaders, who were in such a crucial position to pursue the strategy, were in the end able or willing to act decisively. Either they do not see the main drift — it is too long-term and too theoretical; or they are more concerned to stabilize their own power and position. The preconditions of politically alert labour leaders, vigorous rank and file workers and committed labour intellectuals were scarcely in evidence, from either the survey data or other available information on the union movement. As for labour leaders as members of this strategic elite Mills concludes: 'Never has so much depended upon men who are so ill-prepared and so little inclined to assume responsibility' [37].

The labour leaders then and the trade unions are seen as adaptive organizations rather than a creative source of socialist opposition. In a later article on the same subject, 'The Labor Leaders and the Power Elite', written in 1954, Mills saw no reason to change his view. Within the framework of the existing political economy, he maintained, 'these unions are less levers for change of that general framework than they are instruments for more advantageous integration within it. The drift their actions implement, in terms of the largest projections, is a kind of pro-capitalist syndicalism from the top' [38] .

Let us recall Durkheim's analysis of industrial society. For him the threatening malaise was a breakdown of social order, diagnosed as acute anomie. The problem for the United States, in an advanced industrial society, as seen by Mills, was of an unhealthy social integration — unhealthy because it did not involve the wider public, because it was not therefore thoroughly democratic and because it pointed to the dangerous development of the warfare economy.

There are two observations which can be made in conclusion. First, the concern with the direction of the United States policy — the relation between its economic and political activities — would appear to have some justification in the light of what subsequently happened: the Korean War, the Vietnam War, the Latin American interventions are notable and substantial cases in point. Secondly, the delineation of political publics, while no doubt capable of elaboration and development, is perhaps the most fruitful discussion of publics in Mills's work. In particular, the treatment of the political right enables one to understand some of the ambiguities and conflicts in American politics from Eisenhower to Reagan. Indeed the Reagan administration perhaps gives testimony to the fact that the practical right has more staying power and influence on the main drift than Mills gave it credit for. Rather than war replacing slump as the central threat to American (and world) wellbeing we now have high unemployment in the United States, combined with a highly militaristic stance (albeit with many contradictions and confusions) in world politics. Mills's fears for the future appear to have been well grounded. As for 'the new men of power', at the time of writing some of them are busy preventing steel imports from Europe coming into the USA, whilst the Administration seeks to prevent European firms from fulfilling their contracts to build a gas pipeline from Siberia to Western Europe. We can appreciate why Mills called his alternative programme a 'dream'.

2.6 'WHITE COLLAR'

Estranged from community and Society in a context of distrust and manipulation; alienated from work and, on the personality market, from self; expropriated of individual rationality, and politically apathetic — these are the new little people, the unwilling vanguard of modern society. [39]

> The troubles that confront the white collar people are the troubles of all men and women living in the twentieth century. [40]

These two quotations encapsulate the sombre mood which prevails in *White Collar*. The exaggeration of the second statement leads us to wonder whether we are being offered the secular equivalent of a medieval mystery play for twentieth-century urban men and women. The little person is also the lonely person — that at least is the impression strongly conveyed by the solitary man walking past the skyscraper on the cover of *White Collar*. It is actually the National City Bank on Wall Street. Whether it is a walk into nihilism or whether such people may in the future live fulfilled lives is one of the underlying motifs of the study.

Among other things *White Collar* may be seen as a tract for the times. This is probably what leads Michel Crozier to comment that while it is not a true research study, as a study of the spiritual alienation of the new middle classes, it is Mills's best book: 'A generous spirit infuses his most indignant outburst. Attorney-like he pleads for an image of man which might be considered romantic, but at the same time reveals Mills' ultimate humanity' [41].

Although *White Collar* is a more sprawling book than *The New Men of Power* it is a product of the same period of Mills's life and work and there are important linkages between them. We do not, for example, get the same extended analysis of political publics in *White Collar* but Mills reproduces the same argument about the crucial role of sophisticated conservatives and their working alliance with the trade unions. This is contextualized in the view that liberalism as a movement has moved from active political struggle to an administrative liberalism and has become absorbed by the bureaucratic state. The role of trade unions in counteracting the main drift is again identified. Without such a movement Mills still fears for the future of democracy in America. Essentially it is still the labour movement which Mills thinks could stop America from becoming more and more the kind of society in which 'men are the managed personnel of a garrison state' and who exist within the frenzied order of slump, boom and war' [42].

As a political vanguard the white collar workers looked to be singularly unpromising material to Mills. But they were available and with the exercise of organizational skills plus some political imagination, the labour movement could mobilize the potential power of white collar workers and promote the development of a peaceful industrial society. This is why, given his political diagnosis, Mills talks somewhat desparately about the politics of the rearguard and the need to break through the political indifference of white collar workers.

White Collar was a book which took a long time to complete. There were probably practical and intellectual reasons for this. The 1940s were a busy time for Mills both as a teacher and as an active researcher. The issues eventually to be addressed in the book were mediated partly by his own family background – his father was an insurance agent – and partly by his academic experience as a white collar research worker in a bureaucratic organization.

Despite the negative feelings Mills expresses about research bureaux from time to time, the fact remains that as in the case of *The New Men of Power*, the writing of *White Collar* owes a good deal to the opportunities which membership of such an organization made possible. Among his sources are cited 128 intensive interviews with white collar workers in New York City in 1946, made possible, as he says, by the administrative generosity of Paul Lazarsfeld. From Columbia also he was involved in an intensive study of a Mid-western city. Together with a project which he undertook for the Smaller War Plants Corporation on six cities in the Midwest and New England, this had led to the writing of an article for the *American Sociological Review* as early as 1946: 'The Middle Classes in Middle-Sized Cities'. He also refers in the footnotes to other projects including the survey of Puerto Rican migrants to New York undertaken in 1947, the details of which we look at later. Apart from engagements on other projects putting the empirical material together was time consuming and, in the best sense, opportunistic.

Mills does not parade the technical aspects of the research although the footnotes in *White Collar* are quite informative. There is an interesting note on his use of official statistics. This focuses on the use of occupational categories and their cross-tabulations by income, unemployment and union membership. He explains carefully some of the weaknesses and gaps in the statistics and the basis upon which he decided to re-classify some of the data. The main body of the book does not bristle with statistics, although some of course are woven into the text. This we may speculate was partly to keep the text uncluttered and partly because he did not want to give a spurious objectivity to the study, knowing as he did the limitations of the statistics even after he had done his technical work to make sense of them.

This brings us to another reason which may help to account for the long time *White Collar* took to write, which has to do with his search for an appropriate style of social science. Richard Gillam, in his most perceptive article, 'White Collar from Start to Finish', has reflected upon this:

> The sociologist had come to believe by the late forties that his own discipline, beginning to displace the once dominant 'literature of crisis' as a common denominator of cultural studies, ought to borrow freely from what it aimed to supersede. He thus envisioned *White Collar* as a hybrid work that would combine descriptive accuracy of social science with the emotional force of fiction or even 'poetry'. 'Imagination' would combine competing genres together in a single unitary form. No other work of post-war social analysis, save *The Lonely Crowd,* would attempt so self-consciously to express the 'human meaning' of the 'social facts' in a comparably literary fashion. [43].

This helps to explain Mills's ambivalence to empirical work as traditionally practised. Given that there are technical problems with much data collection — whether social surveys or statistical trend reports — the facts do not speak for themselves. Yet neither can such data be entirely ignored. There are general parameters within which change can be explained and analysed. Some interpretations take on greater plausibility than others even if they can never finally be proved beyond question. The study also reflects of course quite other intellectual debts including Mannheim, Veblen, Cole, Marcuse, and Fromm. Behind all of these stand Marx and Weber. The influence of the 'early' Marx is explicitly acknowledged: Mills's descriptions of salesmen and women selling their labour, which included packaging their own selves and their smiles, are a new application of an old theme. As for Weber many of the concepts are taken direct from him: class, occupation, status, power, authority, bureaucracy and profession are all cases in point.

Yet the introduction to *White Collar* emphasizes the literary allusions to the subject, including among others J. B. Priestley's *Angel Pavement* and George Orwell's *Coming up for Air.* Such writers remind us of the coming into history of the white collar wage earners. In the USA Arthur Miller's *Death of a Salesman* served as a contemporary reference for Mills. Willie Loman is the salesman seized with the American dream of success who, at the end of his life, confused and unhappy, still cannot disbelieve the dream even though his experience and that of his family was a standing refutation of its general efficacy. As a discussion of alienation and false consciousness *White Collar* is the sociological version of Miller's play. There are also perhaps slightly self-conscious allusions to Kafka and Balzac. It leads Mills, for example, to take a phrase of Balzac's — 'insignificant folk cannot be crushed, they lie too flat beneath the foot' — and apply it to the 'lumpen-bourgeoisie'. The bottom of the entrepreneurial world is full of insecurity and unpaid family work in small shops, farms and businesses, people pressed down by economic forces outside their control.

But if the small failing businessman or farmer is the frayed edge of the entrepreneurial class, the new white collar worker is part of the new bureacracies which make up industrial society. Theirs is a greater alienation than that of the traditional proletariat, Mills suggests:

> In the case of the white-collar man, the alienation of the wage worker from the products of his work is carried one step nearer to its Kafka-like completion. The salaried employee does not make anything, although he may handle much that he greatly desires but cannot have. No product of craftsman-ship can be his to contemplate with pleasure as it is being created and after it is made. Being alienated from any pro-duct of his labor, and going year after year through the same paper routine, he turns his leisure all the more frenziedly to the *ersatz* diversion that is sold him, and partakes of the synthetic excitement that neither eases or releases. He is bored at work and restless at play, and this terrible alternative wears him out. [44]

So the lament for the little man and woman in American capitalist society of the twentieth century is really projected to industrial society in general. Surely things must have been better before the advent of the large corporations and the giant bureaucracies which now dominate the social landscape? In developing his critique what Mills is really offering us is a sociological drama with a strong tragic element. He deals in contrasts that have more to do with contrasting images of man than with precise historical analysis. Although the tragic element is strong some hope for the future is indicated — redemption might be possible, although in all truth it is a faint hope. Gillam, a sympathetic expositor, concedes the point:

> Throughout *White Collar*, in fact, Mills writes not as a true historian but rather as a social critic. He quite literally inserts a golden age — a nineteenth century utopia of rationality and freedom — that dramatises what has since been lost. This fails as scholarship but succeeds as radical mythology. His vision of the past, far from being nostalgic or regressive, holds out the possibility that what once existed can be achieved again. What passes as history thus involved a claim to future liberation. [45]

Despite what we have said about the influence of Marx and Weber, in the opening pages of *White Collar* it is the echo of Durkheim that can be heard, although as it happens it is an unacknowledged influence. In the *Division of Labour* Durkheim first confronted the issue of anomie. For all its conceptual sharpness and analytical power, Durkheim's study does not rate highly as a strictly historical account of the transition to industrial society. Yet the diagnosis of the individual isolated from society, of the social currents which feverishly sweep the metropolitan centres causing much anxiety and uncertainty, and of the abnormal forms of the division of labour, still challenges as a critique.

Without mentioning the concept of anomie, Mills offers the following comment which really is an elaboration of its central meaning:

> The uneasiness, the malaise of our time, is due to this root fact: in our politics and economy, in family life and religion — in practically every sphere of our existence — the certainties of the eighteenth and nineteenth centuries have disintegrated or been destroyed and, at the same time, no new sanctions or justifications for the new routines we live, and must live, have taken hold. So there is no acceptance and no rejection, no sweeping hope and no sweeping rebellion. There is no plan of life. Among white collar people, the malaise is deep-rooted; for the absence of any order or belief has left them morally defenceless as individuals and politically impotent as a group. [46]

Of course, the same nineteenth century was the one characterized by Durkheim as anomic. These eighteenth and nineteenth centuries were, we pause to remind ourselves, a period covering the American War of Independence, the French Revolution, the American Civil War and the issue of slavery, the emergence of European socialism and the Darwinian revolution in biology — not forgetting the industrial revolution. In all of this Durkheim appears wiser than Mills. On these grounds *White Collar* does look like a rather flawed product. Is there anything left to be said for it?

If we discount the historical points of reference as in some respects spurious, we are still left with the fact that the twentieth century has been a period of astonishing technological change with occupational and organizational consequences. What Mills does is to focus on some of these features and then offer some models to aid our analysis of what can be observed or construed. We are given accounts of the ways in which the old professions — law, medicine and teaching — are now typically operating in a bureaucratic context. The collegial principle is thus supplanted by the hierarchical. Not only do professionals work with the administrators of these organizations, sometimes they become administrators. So the context in which the 'free professions' live has shifted. Their work has been reorganized in a hierarchical division of labour in which they are paid a salary. Alongside this, Mills depicts the variety of white collar occupations, with some good ethnographical material on the growth of the department store — the Big Bazaar — and the nature of the modern office — the Enormous File.

As for the models, these are the orientating devices which provide anchorage for the study as a whole. There are three key contrasts which we will mention. The first is the contrast between the self-balancing society and the corporate society. The self-balancing society is a model of liberal individualism in a small-scale world of small entrepreneurs and farmers: a decentralized society providing a basis for political democracy. This is the world of early American capitalism with its image of the free man. The corporate state is the labyrinthine, bureaucratic society, with its interlocking connections at the pinnacle of centralized power over which there is no democratic control.

The second contrast is between alienated and non-alienated work. Here Mills uses the model of craftsmanship which we have already encountered. As we have indicated it is not a seriously grounded historical model, although it does nod in the direction of the self-balancing society. Mills has in mind the kind of work which is its own reward and over which the worker exercises control. Through it the worker develops capacities and skills which infuse and give meaning to a way of life. There is no artificial split between work and leisure. The point of this ideal type is to contrast it with the conditions of modern work, where in the detailed division of labour, craftsmanship has been obliterated. Indeed, the craft model is not effectively available to white collar workers and cannot form part of the consciousness even in their imagination. It is so radically different from the world they inhabit that it cannot begin to make sense.

The third contrast has to do with models of political consciousness. Here Mills draws attention to a familiar contrast and then interposes a further possibility. There is the liberal model of the rational individual exercising citizenship rights in pursuit of his or her interests. There is the Marxist class consciousness model in and through which class interests are identified and acted upon collectively. Both models postulate rational behaviour — either individual or collective — in pursuit of defined interests. Yet while such models may be and have been utilized Mills offers the view that the model which most corresponds with the majority of Americans is one representing the absence of political consciousness — namely indifference. He points out that only half of the eligible voters turn out in national elections. Some 50 million do not vote and this constitutes government by default.

How has this political indifference come about? Partly, he thinks, because it is difficult to fight against the powerful when, in the administered state of interlocking bureaucracies, power is anonymous and invisible: 'The problem is who really has power, for often the tangled and hidden system seems a complex yet organised irresponsibility' [47]. Partly it is because the mass media trivialize and make banal the great political events of the day. Whilst, in a general sense, the mass media support the status quo, in that they do not provide a medium for generating counter-symbols, they do not engender active loyalty to the political system: 'The ruling symbols are so inflated in the mass media, the ideological speed-up is so great, that such symbols in their increased volume, intensification and persuasion are worn out and distrusted. The mass media hold a monopoly of the ideologically dead: they spin records of political emptiness' [48].

This political indifference, Mills holds, is also buttressed by the two-party system, which constrains political vision and is helped by the labour unions who, in the economic sphere define their interests and mobilize their resources in relation to the large corporation. This second point is a re-statement of *The New Men of Power* thesis.

If the dice are so heavily loaded against white collar workers — internally fragmented and externally controlled by the impersonal manipulation of their consent, even to the extent of becoming 'cheerful robots' — what hope is there? Are we not simply witnessing and pointing to the inevitable alienation?. Sometimes it looks that way. Indeed, given Mills's general strictures on state socialist bureaucracies elsewhere in his writing, the problem in the end is not simply to be understood as derivative upon monopoly capitalism. At times, Mills's exhortations seem like Wobbly shouts of defiance. Even to shout might be preferable to being manipulated by the powerful without realising it, to being victims of psychical if not material exploitation. But that is only a limited response.

It is the organizational response, involving education to raise the level of awareness together with the growth of a democratic trade union movement, that is called for. This is the route to developing a political consciousness designed to challenge the boom—slump—war economy. It is a thematic statement in Mills's writing which occurs again and again. This involves for its realization a 'cultural struggle' the magnitude of which Mills scarcely under-estimated and whose chances of success he doubted. Nevertheless, it is the possibility of alternatives which stops his thesis of 'main drift' from becoming wholly determinist in character. The powerful with their administrative networks, who sometimes surface from their anonymity in the Millsian category of the sophisticated conservatives, would not easily be dislodged. Mills argued that 'the accumulation of power by any structure is dependent on a triangle of factors: will and know-how, objective opportunity and organisation' [49]. Since these factors interacted, even political in-difference could be overcome and therefore the objective opportunity for transforming American society into more authentically democratic ways remained a possibility. Through his critique Mills sought to put the issue back on the political agenda and not let it go by default.

2.7 THE POWER ELITE

The top of modern American society is increasingly unified and often seems wilfully co-ordinated: at the top there has emerged an elite of power. The middle levels are a drifting set of stalemated balancing forces: the middle does not link the bottom with the top. The bottom of this society is politically fragmented, and even as a passive fact, increasingly powerless: at the bottom there is emerging a mass society. [50]

In this section we will suggest that *The Power Elite* is to be viewed as continuing a discussion of issues and debates already raised in *The New Men of Power* and *White Collar*. In this we disagree with Spinrad who claims that Mills's work is characterized by discontinuity [51]. For example he claims that there is no follow-up from book to book and as an instance of this says that the delineation of 'political publics' in *The New Men of Power* is ignored in later books. Again he says that the problem of work alienation identified in *White Collar* is not taken up in *The Power Elite*. The view taken here is that, on the contrary, the issue of political publics is constantly on Mills's mind even if the full typology is not reproduced in each book. Similarly the question of work alienation could be held to be subsumed in Mills's analysis of mass society in *The Power Elite*. There was no need to repeat what had already been dealt with. This is not to defend Mills against all charges of ambiguity or inconsistency but it is to claim that as the substantive focus of attention changes in each book there are under-lying preoccupations which enable us to see these three studies as a project. Mills himself certainly identified them as a trilogy.

I wrote a book on labor organizations and labor leaders — a politically motivated task; then a book on the middle classes — a task primarily motivated by the desire to articulate my own experience in New York City since 1945. It was thereupon suggested by friends that I ought to round out a trilogy by writing a book on the upper classes. I think the possibility had been in my mind: I had read Balzac off and on during the forties and had been much taken with his self-appointed task of 'covering' all the major classes and types in the society of the era he wished to make his own. [52]

Moreover, in the paragraphs which follow the above quotation, which comes from the Appendix on Intellectual Craftsmanship, in *The Sociological Imagination,* Mills goes on to spell out in some detail how he put the power elite study together. While it necessarily involved innovation and the collection of fresh material, his existing work and materials were quite clearly an important resource. The long-standing interest which Mills had in elite power is clearly revealed in two early review essays. These are 'A Marx for the Managers' (with Hans Gerth) which looks at James Burnham's *The Managerial Revolution* and 'The Nazi Behemoth', a review of Franz Neumann's *Behemoth* [53].

Both essays were originally published in 1942. The first is a strongly stated disagreement with Burnham that 'managers' (a very ambiguously defined term) are emerging as the new elite in both capitalist and communist societies. In particular the idea that because a social group comes to be defined as technically indispensable that therefore they will bid for power and be successful, is rejected. Burnham, it is held, draws the wrong conclusions about the growth of bureaucratic structures in industrial societies. In capitalist societies it should not be assumed that the bureaucrats take over from the capitalists. Always one has to ask who commands the bureaucracy, in whose interests and to what purposes. In the United States, it is suggested, Roosevelt's New Deal actually shored up the system of private property through state regulation and encouraged the growth of the corporate state. This general perspective bears both upon the role of the middle classes in the USA and the dominant ruling groups.

Behemoth was a detailed study of the structure and practice of National Socialism in Germany. Mills is as approving of this book as he is disapproving of Burnham. Neumann describes Nazi Germany as a 'totalitarian monopolistic capitalism'. Four elite groups are identified: the monopoly capitalists, the Nazi Party, the state bureaucracy and the armed forces. 'From these four angles, interests, anchored in the entire social structure but especially in violence and production, coalesce into the central aim: continual preparation and maintenance of imperialist war. To grasp this clearly is to see the structure of the regime as a total thing called Behemoth' [54].

Behemoth served Mills as an examplar of how to analyse social structures. Since this dark European experience records what happened to one form of monopoly capitalism it also speaks of what might happen in the formal democracies of other capitalist countries: 'If you read this book thoroughly, you see the harsh outlines of other possible futures close around you' [55].

From such roots spring *The New Men of Power, White Collar,* and *Power Elite.* There is a fear of a new corporatism: directed by military, industrial and political elites; unopposed by the trade unions following a policy of maximum adaptation to the new corporate order, overcoming the interests of the 'old' middle classes; and untroubled by the 'new' middle class, which is full of status anxieties and empty of class consciousness. This new corporatism points in the direction of a war economy by way of handling the slump—boom cycle. All of this suggests to Mills the danger of a mass society being created, moving in the direction of a totalitarian society. The continuity of this thematic preoccupation can be clearly seen from the early 1940s on. The counter-theme to this is a concern that the USA approach more closely its democratic ideals with lively educated publics represented by an accountable peace-oriented leadership: this recurs throughout the trilogy. The worry was that anti-democratic trends could occur behind people's backs and would go unrecognized, because the rhetoric of democracy and the trappings of formal democracy would be falsely identified with the real thing.

The idea of a democratic society commonly carries with it the concept of political leaders who are representative of, and accountable to the electors. Together with this is the concept of checks and balances whereby co-existing and competing groups in society prevent tyranny and ensure political and economic freedom. Power is diffused and de-centralized and groups compete on the basis of approximate parity. Such a situation never existed but Mills writes of the romantic pluralism of the Jeffersonian ideal in the pre-Civil War period as a balancing society, as we have already seen in *Sociology and Pragmatism* and *White Collar.* It appears in *The Power Elite.* He is well aware that the clock cannot be turned back but his argument in part is that the pluralism which exists in modern American society is a much more subdued affair. The political and economic orders are no longer autonomous but are fused within an enlarged state apparatus. This centralization and linkage of orders to which can be added the military order, results in a growing asymmetry of power relations. Hence the concept of the balance of power in society as a whole is not grounded in reality. In this respect Mills disagrees with pluralistic writers like David Rieseman, who advanced the thesis that in the United States pluralism is alive and well in the form of 'veto groups'. For Rieseman the problem at the top of American society was not that there was too much power, but an undirected drift − an impotent leadership rather than a power elite [56]. He also disagrees with J. K. Galbraith's view of countervailing power insofar as it implies a power balance. In fact, as expressed in *American Capitalism,* there are many qualifications at the empirical level to this thesis and Mills is right to draw attention to them. Further, as he points out, it is a normative theory put forward by Galbraith to guide public policy rather than a statement describing how things are. The Galbraith thesis, then, should be regarded as a form of ideological hope born of liberal aspirations and as such represents a possible image of the future rather than a present reality. Mills's point is that such pluralist tendencies as do exist in American society are insufficient to ensure a healthy democracy.

Linked with this version of what might be called subdued pluralism − groups and associations who cannot restrain the power elite − is a view about the transformation of a community of publics into a society of masses. The contrast can be presented in the following way:

Community of publics	*Society of masses*
1. Virtually as many people express opinions as receive them.	1. Far fewer people express opinions than receive them. Individuals receive impressions from the mass media.
2. Public communications provide the opportunity for opinions to be replied to publicly and quickly.	2. It is difficult or impossible for individuals to answer back immediately or with any effect.
3. Opinion can be mobilized into action if necessary against prevailing authority	3. The realization of opinion in action is controlled by authorities who organize and control the channels of such action.
4. Authoritative institutions do not penetrate the public which therefore has autonomy of operation.	4. The mass has no autonomy from authorized institutions and this affects opinion formation itself.

This perceived undermining of the community of democratic publics, as Mills sometimes calls them, is related to the growth of the mass media. These can, he believes, transform publics into media markets who are passively exposed to their contents and are extremely vulnerable to manipulation. The community of publics, as a source of diverse opinion and critical, effective responses to authority (which is thereby more accountable) has, as it were, been expropriated by the centralized organization of communication. Such media do not allow the individual to connect his or her life with national and world events. They do not provide insight into nor a rational understanding of larger realities: they obscure them and are a distraction. Moreover, the media themselves are available to elites to exploit through propaganda, public relations and the management of news and opinion. Manipulation as a technique is antithetical to democracy. The strategy of manipulation is to persuade people that they have made decisions, when in fact they have not. Mills sees this as a weapon employed by the power elite: persuasion also involves the screening out of possible counter-opinions.

Mills is pointing to a trend rather than an absolute state of affairs (which, were it to be realized, would be a totalitarian state). He wishes to put what weight he has as an educator and communicator to counter-act these trends, which by hostile critics can be interpreted as a kind of quixotic activity. But the role of the intellectual here is seen as breathing some life into dying publics and thereby taking part in the cultural struggle.

Mills deliberately uses the concept of power elite rather than ruling class. For this reason he is sometimes criticized by Marxist writers notwithstanding their general sympathy to much of what he has to say [57]. He takes the view that 'ruling class' theories assume that an economic class rules politically and that the concept does not allow enough autonomy to the political order, neither does it give a clear reference to the role of the military. He suggests that those who hold command posts in each of these institutional orders have a definite autonomy but that in intricate ways important decisions are made which involve a measure of coalescence.

The opportunity for such a power elite to emerge in a formally democratic country is traced back to institutional trends within the political, economic and military orders and the growing coincidence of their objective interests. The men who occupy the top posts in each order (and they are usually men not women) are seen as being broadly similar in social background and outlook. At the same time Mills makes a distinction between the inner core of the power elite and its outer fringes. By inner core he means those who interchange commanding roles at the top of one institutional order with those in another. Examples offered are the admiral who is also a banker, a lawyer who leads an important federal commission, an executive head of a corporation supplying war materials who becomes Secretary of Defence, and a wartime general who becomes a civilian member of the political directorate, within the executive breach of government, and then becomes a member of the board of directors of a leading economic corporation. This movement from one institutional milieu to another helps to bind the power elite together since the particularities of interests of one institutional order are transcended. To such men should be added top corporation lawyers and investment bankers who are top level link people between one elite order and another. The outer fringes of the power elite are more fluid and less easily defined, but Mills refers to the technical lieutenants of power, such as administrative assistants, speech writers and public relations men.

The view put forward in *The Power Elite* is that interlocking elites are operating especially for the benefit of the military. This has led to the general adoption of a 'military metaphysic' within the United States such that foreign policy has tended to be defined in terms of military necessity. The significance of the American power elite, therefore, is that foreign policy happens over the heads of the people, including their elected representatives, and that policy which is so fateful for the well-being of the world tends to be oriented to a warlike posture. For this reason the power elite is judged to be in a more powerful position than any other group in history, given the possible consequences of the decisions they make or fail to make.

Mills not only attempts to delineate the power elite, he also indicts them. This reaches a climax in the last chapter of the book, entitled 'The Higher Immorality'. They are, he insists, neither representative nor responsible in their positions and use of power:

America ... appears now before the world a naked and arbitrary power, as, in the name of realism, its men of decision enforce their often crackpot decisions upon world reality. The second-rate mind is in command of the ponderously spoken platitude. In the liberal rhetoric, vagueness, and in the conservative mood, irrationality, are raised to principle. Public relations and the official secret, the trivialising campaign and the terrible fact clumsily accomplished, are replacing reasoned debate of political ideas in the privately incorporated economy, the military ascendancy, and the political vacuum of modern America. [58]

Mills fully expected *The Power Elite* to be regarded as a controversial thesis and in some respects he knew that he was going beyond what he could conclusively demonstrate. He hoped that by not taking the world for granted and exploring a significant issue with such materials as he could assemble, he would promote a reasoned dialogue that would unmask some untruths and lead to a better understanding of contemporary reality. There are times, perhaps, when in addition to the absence of corroborating evidence there are some blurred edges in the argument. He can deflect either/or dichotomies into both/and statements just at the point when sharp clarification is sometimes called for. For example, is the power elite visible? It is not entirely hidden, but it is not altogether surfaced. The conditions for or the extent of visibility are not clearly specified. Again, do those who hold key command posts always make key decisions? They can and they might; sometimes they might not actively decide anything; but this does not tell us anything about decision-making as such only about the social arena within which the process takes place. Do elites consciously conspire to achieve their ends? Not really, but conspiracies do happen. Are we to assume an impersonal administered state controlling the masses or definite people making big decisions with world-wide consequences? Both. There are structures which are the product of historical drift, especially exemplified in large bureaucracies, but there are agents who wilfully plan to do things from high positions of power under the protection of secrecy and/or in a context of managed public relations. If the proper answer to some of these questions is both rather than either/or then some sense of which part of the answer applies to which particular circumstances needs to be spelled out.

Critical discussions of *The Power Elite* are of various kinds: empirical, analytical, interpretative and political. We will indicate now some of the lines they take.

Of particular interest is a long review essay by Talcott Parsons, 'The Distribution of Power in the United States' [59]. Incidentally this essay is far removed from the jargon-ridden prose of *The Social System*, which Mills was later to lampoon in *The Sociological Imagination*. Parsons sees the book as 'a subtle and complex combination of acceptable and unacceptable elements' [60] and places Mills in the Veblen tradition of social criticism. He doubts that Mills has made a convincing case. In his judgement Mills has downgraded the role of the political parties and diminished the tangible link between the presidency and the party system. Likewise the role of the judiciary is unfairly played down, bearing in mind its re-assertion of civil rights in the wake of McCarthyism and its record on race relations judgements on the segregation issue. Not all lawyers are instruments of business corporations. Although Mills appears to operate in a long-term perspective Parsons thinks that there is a tendency to generalize from recent short-term developments. In particular the role of the military is cited. Parsons agrees that in recent years the military ascendancy has existed but suggests that things are changing. He does not, however, develop this point save to assert that the structure of American political leadership is not settled. Parsons further doubts that the 'mass society' element is so pronounced in the USA as Mills thinks, arguing this point with reference to the role of kinship, friendship and associational groups (noting particularly the growth in church membership).

Parsons disagrees fundamentally with Mills's treatment of power. It is, he says, a 'zero-sum' view (a phrase Mills does not employ) which defines power as power over others and at the expense of others. In other words, Mills concentrates on the distributive aspects of power — who has power, in whose interests and for what purposes — and not in how power is generated as a facility in the social system whereby things get done on behalf of society as a whole, in the general interest. This, suggests Parsons, is partly because Mills has a utopian ideal of a society in which power plays no part. There are grounds for thinking that Mills does have an ambivalent attitude to power in society because he does not like to come to terms with society as a system of domination. In an autobiographical note he once confessed:

> I am a Wobbly. But do you know what a Wobbly is? It's a kind of spiritual condition ... Wobbly is not only a man who takes orders from himself. He's also a man who's often in the situation where there are no regulations to fall back upon, which he hasn't made up himself. He doesn't like bosses, capitalistic or communistic, they're all the same to him. He wants to be, and he wants everyone else to be, his own boss at all times under all conditions and for any purposes they want to follow up. This kind of spiritual condition, and only this, is Wobbly freedom. [61]

However, if that is the romantic idealist, the pragmatist in him combines with a liberal-socialist political perspective to recognize the reality of power and to consider how the democratic ideals of responsible and responsive leadership may be approximated in a framework of public accountability. Against Parson's optimism about the temporary ascendancy of the military, and his view that the main lines of social development are essentially acceptable to a humanistic ethic, Mills offers a more Manichean view, accompanied by a residual hope that a democratic transformation might nonetheless take place.

With the benefit of hindsight we can say that since 1956 the military ascendancy is still with us and Parsons's point about over-generalizing from the short term looks less convincing. Even at the time, however, there were reasonable gounds for Mills to take World War II and the subsequent Cold War period as marking a profound shift in the organization of structural power. We will return again to the question of the military—industrial complex in discussing *The Causes of World War III* and in the conclusion.

For the moment we may note that whether the military are co-equal in a trinity of elite power is another matter. Miliband, for example, thinks that the role of the military in Mills's analysis is somewhat exaggerated. He thinks that its effective power base is not so strong as the economic elite. Further, if the role of the military in policy forma-tion is overstated, it may deflect attention away from civilian power-holders in the state [62]. Mills, one suspects, did not want to be unduly dogmatic here. It is the growth of the military order and its inter-penetration with the political and economic orders which he emphasizes. What he resists is the idea of economic determinism or any other determinism, save as a heuristic device.

Another critic, coming from a somewhat different angle, is Daniel Bell. In *The End of Ideology* he reviews *The Power Elite* in an essay entitled, 'Is There a Ruling Class in America? *The Power Elite* Recon-sidered'. Another relevant essay in the same volume is, 'America as a Mass Society'. His general view, as represented in the second essay is that the concept of mass society (with its varying definitions) does not connect adequately with the complex relations found in industrial societies such as the USA. Mass society is simply used as a large-scale abstraction, which carries diagnoses that are meaningless without standards of comparison. The concept of mass society has become, he suggests, simply an ideology of romantic protest against contemporary life. He seems to think that it is not appropriate anyway to import European concepts to explain American society, which seems a rather extreme version of American exceptionalism.

Bell thinks Mills is too preoccupied with the role of power in society, especially with its violent manifestations. Yet power may indeed have violent manifestations and outcomes, as in war. Mills in any case, as we have seen, is interested in the co-existence of power as subtle manipulation, which is not violent in form at all. Rather it is the massaging of consent.

Bell further claims that the argument for a power elite rests on the idea of an explicit community and continuity of interests between the various segments. Moreover, he claims, the mechanisms of co-ordination have to be established and then accountability or non-accountability demonstrated rather than asserted. What Mills has failed to do, he suggests, is to discuss decision-making in any concrete way. If this were done, much more attention would need to be given to the 'middle level' groups and then the extent to which an actual elite was cohesive and independent of these middle levels would become clearer. A similar point was also made by Parsons and also by Gracey and Anderson in a long review article. The latter maintain that Mills does not examine the career of specific legislative programmes and insist that the Eisenhower administration had to abandon its farm programme as a result of lobby pressure [63]. The power of the farm lobby over the years does seem well illustrated by the continuing shipment of grain to the Soviet Union even at the present time when the Polish question has resulted in trade embargoes.

Bell's critique is as robust as Mills's own writing. At times though he overdoes the case for the prosecution. For example, he claims that Mills completely evades discussion of the Cold War and of the extent to which the American posture is shaped by the Russians. The question of how to respond to Soviet intentions was not, he says, a decision of the power elite, but a judgement derived from scholarly appraisals like George Kennan's and the policy-planning staff of the State Department:

> It was a judgement that Stalinism as an ideological phenomenon, and Russia as a geo-political power, were aggressively, militarily and ideologically expansionist, and that a policy of containment, including a rigid military build-up was necessary in order to implement that commitment. This underlay Truman's Greco-Turkish policy, and it underlay the Marshall Plan and the desire to aid the re-building of the European economy. These policies were not a reflex of power constellations within the United States. They were estimates of national interest and national survival. [64]

This does seem to be a very concise statement of American foreign policy during this period but Mills's point is precisely that international relations have come to be dominated by military considerations. This does not absolve the Soviet Union from its militarism and this is a matter which is taken up emphatically in *The Causes of World War III*. His central point about American foreign policy in *The Power Elite* was that it heightened rather than reduced tension and for that precise reason is dangerous:

The American elite does not have any real image of peace — other than as an uneasy interlude existing precariously by virtue of the balance of mutual fright. The only seriously accepted plan for 'peace' is the fully loaded pistol. In short, war or a high state of war-preparedness is felt to be the normal and seemingly permanent condition of the United States. [65]

When, therefore, Bell describes *The Power Elite* as a 'political book whose loose texture and power rhetoric have allowed different people to read their own emotions into it' [66] we must recognize that his emotions also were not untouched.

There have been other, more sympathetic critiques. William Domhoff, in *The Higher Circles*, clearly regards a number of his essays as a fleshing out of the power elite thesis. These include essays on American foreign policy, domestic policy and social legislation, as well as what he refers to as the seamy side of the power elite, the CIA [67]. Herbert Aptheker, in *The World of C. Wright Mills*, thinks that the power difference between the elite and the masses, postulated by Mills, should be qualified:

In whole areas of life — as in wages and working conditions, housing and education, the battle against Jim Crow and against war — the desires and the power of the masses do exert great influence, manifested in buses that stop running and in atomic bombs that, though loaded aboard planes that are alerted to take off, never are dropped in war. [68]

Since Mills's death things have happened which count for and against his thesis. The prosecution of the Vietnam war and the bombing of Cambodia were elitist decisions, yet the anti-war movement, which received some support from the media as in the case of the My Lai massacre, brought the troops back home. Watergate again showed the seamy side of elite power, but it was uncovered and the judiciary, the media and the Senate can take some credit for the removal of President Nixon from office. The constitutional checks and balances could be said to be slow moving and painful but they did work in some measure. What can be said is that Mills's portrayal, even if exaggerated and not always substantiated, did stimulate social scientists to look again at a world that they had too long taken for granted. Above all there is a moral conviction that infuses *The Power Elite*: it is that the state exists to serve us not to dominate us and take away our freedom.

2.8 THE LATIN-AMERICAN CONNECTION: 'PUERTO RICAN JOURNEY' AND 'LISTEN YANKEE'

Puerto Rican Journey was published in 1950 and *Listen Yankee: the Revolution in Cuba* in 1960. They are very different books in style and purpose but what they have in common is a sense of the interdependency which exists between the USA and Latin America, including in this the Spanish Caribbean. Both studies remind us of the asymmetrical economic and political linkages which the United States has had with Latin American client cultures. The first study tells us something about the management of the immigrant labour market and its social consequences for the Puerto Rican migrant. The second book discusses how and why Cuba came to break the client relationship with the United States and reflects on the significance of this for both parties.

Puerto Rican Journey was written with Clarence Senior and Rose Goldsen. Mills was the director of the research study on which the book was based. The work was done during Mills's time at Columbia's Bureau of Applied Social Research. The centrepiece of the study was an interview programme with 1,113 Puerto Rican households in Spanish Harlem and Morrisania, New York. Given that the household was the unit, information pertaining to some 5,000 Puerto Ricans was obtained. Sixty-five interviewers were employed, most of whom were Puerto Ricans. In addition government and state officials in New York, Washington DC and San Juan were interviewed together with the heads of social and welfare agencies.

Unlike *The New Men of Power*, *Puerto Rican Journey* does carry an appendix with the interview questions. In some respects the interview schedule is ambitious. There are 101 questions, many of them subdivided. Some of the ground covered is typical of such surveys. How long has the interviewee lived in New York? How did they learn about New York in Puerto Rico? Why did they come? What jobs had they held, if any, before coming? What was their present employment position? How did they get their present job? How do they see their occupational future? How do they see their children's future? There were also questions about the use of the mass media, about forms of socializing and about the care of and facilities for children.

There were curious questions like: Do any children living in this house take cod liver oil? There were other questions about social security arrangements, the use of welfare agencies and relations with the law, which, one suspects, might well have led to evasive answers. In the middle of a very long schedule there was a very Millsian question: Everybody occasionally has troubles: has anything in particular been troubling you lately? Perhaps the interviewer was the latest in a long list of troubles.

Interviewers were also instructed to observe physical type with a five category distinction — white, indio, grifo, mulatto, negro. They were asked in addition to classify the respondent with respect to skin colour (four choices) hair (kinky, wavy, straight) lips (thick, medium, thin) and nose (narrow—thin, medium and broad—fleshy). This gives it all a somewhat period flavour and, truth to tell, one is surprised to find it.

According to Robert Blauner, in a more recent essay,

> The lower structure of the American working class has become predominantly Afro-American, Mexican-American and Puerto Rican. Suffering high rates of unemployment and marginal employment, third world workers fit Marx's conception of an industrial reserve army, which meets the system's needs for an elastic labour pool. When working they tend to be concentrated in jobs that are insecure, dirty, unskilled and at the bottom of the hierarchy of authority where there is little possibility for advancement. [69]

This comment precisely mirrors the substance of Mills and Senior's findings so far as the Puerto Ricans were concerned. Many of the migrants were women, many black, both of which categories often reinforced by language problems, were disadvantageous in the labour market. Moreover, they reported that the opportunities for upwards occupational mobility were slowing down and that migrants scaled down their aspirations in the light of experience. Mills and Senior put it this way:

> By living at a similar class level, in the same regions of the city, doing the same type of work, having the same type of troubles, being exposed to the same type of mass communications, their imaginative life becomes leveled out. In their day-to-day struggle, absorbed in the need to function inconspicuously with a minimum of psychic discomfort, they have little time left over for thought about the future. [70]

The reference to functioning inconspicuously really means surviving without coming to the attention of the authorities or 'causing trouble' to the 'host society'. Mills and Senior comment on this notion of 'adaptation' through assimilation', which had characterized American race relations studies under the notable influence of Robert Park. Such assimilation, they suggest, cannot realistically be achieved any more upward mobility to any great extent. What one is actually talking about is survival at the bottom of the pile and that is difficult to do 'inconspicuously'. The authors also cite the ideology of cultural pluralism as an alternative to the 'melting pot' assimilationist thesis. This emphasizes cultural diversity as a value rather than the necessity of adjusting to a supposedly homogenous host society. While the tolerance of different ethnic life styles may be a good liberal doctrine, Mills and Senior suggest that the reality of the immigrants' experience is something else. This is because, despite the officially espoused values of America as the land of the free, which provides a welcome to the outcast and the downtrodden, there remains a migration rhetoric, used by the press and some politicians, which defines the new arrivals, whoever they are, as a threat and as undesirably different. The reality of life becomes one where there are sharp ethnic conflicts and a struggle to survive at the margins of a society where the American dream for these migrants is only an absurd fantasy.

Puerto Rican Journey does then point to the weaknesses of 'melting pot' and 'cultural pluralist' theories without developing a fully fledged alternative. It conveys an understanding that there are general features about the waves of migration to the USA and an accompanying anti-migrant rhetoric, whilst insisting that for cultural, economic and structural reasons the problems of the Puerto Rican migrants in the mid-twentieth century were particularly acute: 'The Puerto Ricans must be classed as part of 'the new immigrants' many of whose members have not followed the classic pattern with the ease some liberal commentators suppose, or, indeed, have not followed it at all' [71] To that extent the study anticipates the more radical analysis of race relations taken up by Robert Blauner some twenty years later, where the emphasis is on institutionalized racism and where the ghettoes are seen as evidence of cultural oppression and economic exploitation [72]. Clearly, however, more recent history suggests that the fatalistic, resigned attitudes to experienced realities has been replaced by more active resistance and rebellion and the assertion of Spanish-American culture.

One thing which Mills, Senior and Goldsen do bring out very clearly is the asymmetrical relationship between Puerto Rico and the United States. The island has the status of a client culture, having been ceded by Spain to the United States in 1898. Its political status and the electoral rights of its citizens remained ambiguous for a long time. As a plantation economy, based on sugar, its population was poor, landless and undernourished. Migration to New York was defined in terms of economic necessity and as a response to an available opportunity. But, as Mills, Senior and Goldsen show, it was the business cycle which effectively regulated migration flows. They point out that from 1908 to 1948 the correlation between the ups and downs of the physical volume of business activity on the continent and the waves and troughs of Puerto Rican migration registered the high coefficient of 0.73 [73]. The relationship between a poor plantation economy and an advanced industrial society is thus established and serves as something of a paradigmatic example of the relationship between the first and third world. This provides the connecting point between the Puerto Rican study and the very differently presented *Listen Yankee*, written a decade later, to which we now turn.

Listen Yankee is not an academic sociological study. Mills himself regarded it as a pamphlet: 'My major aim in this book,' he wrote, 'is to present the voice of the Cuban revolutionary as clearly and as emphatically as I can; and I have taken up this aim because of its absurd absence from the news of Cuba available in the United States'. [74] Apart from some brief preparatory work the substance of the matter is the product of a few weeks' stay in Cuba. This included some very extended conversations with Fidel Castro and many of the key officials in the new administration, including Ché Guevara, the President of the National Bank of Cuba and Oswaldo Torrado, the Cuban President. All this was written in a few weeks, was published in the same year and ran into several reprints. The book consists of a brief introduction followed by eight 'letters' in which Mills uses direct speech to convey a composite picture of how the Cuban revolutionaries see their revolution, how they define their aspirations and their relationships with the United States and the Soviet Union. There is a final note to the reader in which Mills states his own personal views on the Cuban revolution.

As a piece of 'alternative journalism' *Listen Yankee* is a vigorous and provocative statement. He did not incidentally attribute the absence of this missing point of view from the American press to a capitalist plot, or even to the pressures of advertisers, but rather as something which was a product of ignorance and confusion among journalists — a failure of understanding and imagination. While even to express the alternative view in the United States was bound to be controversial, there were public figures like Eleanor Roosevelt who were ready to acknowledge that, although the Cuban views may not be liked, they should be attended to with care.

In his study, *Modern Revolutions*, John Dunn reminds us that 'Cuba did become to a very considerable degree an economic colony of the United States, as Guevara and others complained. It was a prototype for the most offensive style of neo-colonialism, a relationship in which American governments intervened persistently in Cuban internal affairs in order to favour the interests of American citizens' [75]. Mills was well aware of this and of the history of relationships between the United States and Latin America generally. He knew that the Monroe Doctrine, originally intended to keep European colonists out of the Americas in the nineteenth century, had become an instrument of United States hegemony. We may recall, although Mills does not comment on it, the deep-rooted ideology of manifest destiny in the United States, which asserted the special mission of the (white) United States to extend its benevolent influences to the whole American continent. Walt Whitman had indeed urged the annexation of Cuba by the United States as early as 1846 on just such grounds. That did not happen, but after the Spanish—American war of 1898 Cuba was subject to United States control. Even after the formation of the Republic of Cuba in 1903, the island was subject to the Platt Amendment, which gave the USA the right to intervene to protect Cuban 'independence'. This they did from time to time during the twentieth century to protect American owned banking, sugar and tobacco interests.

The Batista regime which Castro eventually toppled in 1959, had been well supplied with arms, planes and bombs. Batista's troops were trained by American Military Missions, Given the torture and corruption with which the regime was associated, the USA's actions were seen by the Cuban revolutionaries as imperialist. Moreover, this kind of control and intervention characterized much of United States policy towards Latin America and the Carribbean. Between 1895 and 1933, for example there were thirty such interventions. Since World War II the policy has been maintained with the added ideological ingredient of keeping communism at bay. There was the Guatemalan intervention in 1964. Mills's book appeared before the abortive Bay of Pigs invasion planned by the CIA in conjunction with Cuban exiles in the USA, and sanctioned by President Kennedy. This kind of episode was recognized as a very real possibility by Mills and the Cubans because that, after all, was consistent with the record of the United States in Latin America.

Part of Mills's purpose in writing was to argue against such policies. He suggested that overt hostility and the development of sanctions against Cuba would drive the new, independent, socialist state out of a neutralist stance and into the Soviet bloc, which, as we now know, is precisely what happened. The possibility of Cuba becoming a base for Soviet rockets was touched upon by Mills and again, as we know, the issue became the focus of the missile crisis in 1962. At the same time, the existence of American bases in Turkey, on the Soviet Union's borders, did not, Mills observed, give the United States a strong moral position in the argument.

Mills saw the significance of the new Cuban revolution as an opportunity for the United States to rethink its foreign policy in relation to third world aid, cold war strategy and Latin-American containment. This has not happened. Despite occasional thaws, Cuba still remains defined as a hostile neighbour. Elsewhere in Latin America the policy of intervention has been pursued in Nicaragua, El Salvador and of course in Chile, where President Allende's constitutionally elected communist government was toppled in an American supported coup.

There are two general points about Mills's own stance to the Cuban revolution, which offer more general guidance to his own value position. First, he was clearly sympathetic to the revolution. This was in part simply because he thought the Cuban people deserved better than Batista and his oppressive regime. Moreover, he regarded it as an intellectual default not to see the possibilities in this new society, even whilst he recognized and had reservations about a society being so dependent upon a charismatic leader. That is to say, one could be for the revolution and, at the same time, fear possible outcomes like the emergence of a new tyranny or a war-oriented economy sucked into the Cold War conflict. To assume that as a necessary outcome was, Mills thought, a world-weary response of intellectuals who cannot think through the positive implications of revolutionary movements for change in the third world. For Mills the possibilities contained in the revolution appealed to the romantic and the pragmatist in him. The romantic could marvel at the Castro victory against incredible odds and the unbureaucratic way in which new beginnings were made. The pragmatist in him could see that there was a real job to be done and real problems to be solved. Manifestly he took pleasure in the role that intellectuals had played in the revolutionary movement. If revolution is construction then perhaps there was a place for his ideal of craftsmanship in the new society — including a place for intellectual craftsmen.

Secondly, Mills reveals a generally dissenting, non-conformist attitude to society. While he thought liberalism was outmoded as a social force, as a personal stance for the individual it retained significance for him. In his concluding note he cites Hobhouse's splendid text *Liberalism* and says that, like Hobhouse, he cannot give unconditional loyalty to any institution, man, state, movement or nation. This for him is the intellectual base point for the social critic. It is the ground of his position against those who would attack him for being unpatriotic to the United States. In one sense he was reminding Americans of their own revolutionary tradition rooted in the right to dissent.

Nor should we forget the other side of the coin. Even in relation to revolutions with which one was in sympathy and to which one was committed, it is always necessary to safeguard space for critique. This is a necessary check against tyranny and against complacency.

2.9 'THE CAUSES OF WORLD WAR III'

All significant problems of contemporary man and society bear upon the issue of war and the politics of peace; and the solution to any significant problem in some part rests upon their outcome. [76]

The Causes of World War III was first published in 1958 and then updated and re-issued in 1960 (quotations in this text are from the 1960 edition). This radical pamphlet was written by a sociologist deeply committed to the cause of peace and disarmament. There is a sharp, challenging edge to the whole statement, which gives it something of the character of a sermon. Mills sometimes wryly acknowledges his preacher's style. One part of the book is actually headed, 'A Pagan Sermon'. This was a strong word to the Christian clergy in the USA to take seriously their faith and not accommodate to the warfare state.

Do not these times demand a little Puritan defiance? Do not they demand the realization of how close hell is to being a sudden and violent reality in man's world today? Should not those who have access to the peoples of Christendom stand up and denounce with all the righteousness, and pity and anger and charity and love of humility their faith may place at their command, the political and militarist assumptions now followed by the leaders of the nations of Christendom? Should they not denounce the pseudo-religiosity of men of high office who would steal religious phrases to decorate crackpot policies and immoral lack of policies ... Should they not realize that the positive moral meaning of what is called 'neutralism' lies in the resolve that the fate of mankind shall not be determined by the idiotically conducted rivalry of the United States and the Soviet Union? [77]

After he wrote, more voices were raised in the anti-war movement opposed to American policy in Vietnam. More recently the peace movement in the United States and Europe appears to have found its voice. At the time of writing the Church of England has come out with a working party report, *The Church and the Bomb*, which Mills would surely have applauded [78].

Mill's challenge was related to his view that there was a tremendous moral force to be tapped and that there was a public which could be aroused by courageous leadership. If the challenge was not taken up then Christianity would be in default of its message: passivity on the issue of war and peace is to be a spectator of humanity's moral defeat. Consciousness-raising could be undertaken by intellectual groups who are prepared to communicate with a large public a message of resistance to war-oriented national policies.

In a similar way Mills called upon scientists to behave as moral beings, who are responsible for what they do. They should not shelter behind the military and governmental bureaucracies and become part of a secret Science Machine based on national difinitions of security. He recognized that some scientists were indeed conscious of the political implications of working on weapons development — including chemical and biological weapons as well as nuclear bombs. Again, however, the concern was that the individual issue of the scientist's conscience should take on a public dimension. 'Scientists should establish their own private forums and public outlets. For the time is over-ripe for an intensified and responsible communication between scientists and other cultural workmen, and between scientists and larger publics' [79]. Through public communication their contribution can become politically relevant and prevent them from being used as hired people of the ruling circles. This is what makes scientists socially responsible and not servants of elite power. Secret science, in Mills's view, is a contradiction in terms. Open science not only encourages a democratic spirit but in some measure reduces insecurity and anxiety in international relations and also diminishes the control of scientific work by irresponsible elites.

The norm of secrecy was accompanied by worries over 'atom spies' and breaches of security and hence the need for 'clearing' scientists who would handle 'classified' information. In periods of cold war such matters take on an obsessive character. However, it is worth recalling the initiatives of prominent scientists like Bertrand Russell, Albert Einstein and Linus Pauling who began the Pugwash Movement in 1955. This is described by Russell in *Has Man a Future?* [80]. The purpose was precisely to secure co-operation between Communist and non-Communist scientists in recognition of the threat that nuclear weapons posed for the whole world.

The Pugwash Conferences were seen as an international forum in which scientists could communicate across ideological barriers. They could also warn the nations of the world in authoritative terms what the consequences of nuclear war would be. Nowadays in the USA and in Europe the voice of scientists are more frequently heard warning the general public about the medical, ecological and physical effects of nuclear weapons and counteracting official government propaganda. The formation of Scientists Against Nuclear Arms in Britain, in 1980, is an example of the kind of thing Mills was calling for two decades ago.

Although *The Causes of World War III* was the first time Mills focused so centrally on the war and peace question, we have already seen that it was never far from his thoughts. This is obviously the case in *The Power Elite* and it is fair to say that a good deal of the framework of *The Causes of World War III* is derivative upon that study. But Mills also refers explicitly back to *The New Men of Power* and the discussion of the trend toward a permanent war economy. The pace and tactics of this development he saw as being affected by the phases of the slump—war—boom cycle. But the general diagnosis, we may briefly recall, is of the practical rightists (broadly, the smaller business groups) pursuing policies that lead to slump and then effectively being taken over by the sophisticated conservatives (broadly, big business and finance capital) whose policy making is war-oriented. This, he claims, is exactly what was happening during the Eisenhower administration.

Not that Eisenhower was happy with the state of affairs. Mills quotes the fact that in 1959 Eisenhower expressed concern about the role of financial interests and the munitions lobby in determining defence policy issues. Two years later, in his farewell address as President, he spoke of his fears about the military—industrial complex:

> In the councils of government, we must guard against the acquisition of unwarranted influence, whether sought or unsought, by the military—industrial complex. The potential for the disastrous rise of misplaced power exists and will persist. We must never let the weight of this combination endanger our liberties or democratic processes. We should take nothing for granted. Only an alert and knowledgeable citizenry can compel the proper meshing of the huge industrial and military machinery of defence with our peaceful methods and goals, so that security and liberty may prosper together. [81]

Mills does tend to focus on the USA in his discussion. This is because he thinks that as an American he has a particular responsibility to counter the hostile images of the Soviet Union and the conventional wisdom about the Soviet threat to the 'free world'. He sees the USSR too as ruled by a power elite and plainly refers to its brutality, tyranny and absence of freedom. But it is the 'fearful symmetry' between the two great nations which creates a mutual suspicion and feeds the arms race, in his view. They may have different ideologies — capitalism and communism. They may be at different stages of economic development and embody different cultures. But they share too closely the military metaphysic.

Given the interlocking features which define the arms race, Mills does not seriously attempt to apportion out the balance of blame. He does, however, remind American readers by way of a correction to cold war journalism, that the Soviet Union lost twenty million people in the Second World War, and that, for them, the German question is a particularly sensitive one. Moreover, on the record are a number of Soviet peace initiatives. The Soviets stopped nuclear tests unilaterally and made a number of specific disarmament proposals. At the beginning of the book Mills refers to the Paris Summit of 1960 when the Eisenhower—Kruschev talks were broken off after the Russians shot down a U2 spy plane over their own territory. President Eisenhower publicly accepted responsibility for the flight, which had, it was also admitted, been going on for a number of years. Mills's purpose here was simply to draw attention to facts and events which his fellow Americans might scarcely know, or have glossed over. In the end though he maintains that, while one country or another may be blamed for particular things, the strategic causes of World War III lie in the lethal symmetry of action.

This general approach has much in common with E. P. Thompson's recent influential essay, 'Notes on Exterminism: the Last Stage of Civilisation' [82]. Thompson cites Mills early in his essay, making particular references to what Mills had termed the drift and thrust towards World War III. These two concepts are central to Mills's analysis since they try and deal with the perennially knotty problem of structure and agency in social change. Unless some place is left for human agency historical inevitability the product of uncontrollable structural forces, dominates any analysis. Yet Mills is crucially concerned to distinguish between 'fate' understood as a consequence of inescapable structural forces and 'fate' as a social construct, in which authorities assure us that nothing else can be done, that present policies are 'necessary' and 'realistic' and that there is no alternative that is 'practical'. While we may be persuaded or manipulated into believing that what these authorities say is true, it is not the same kind of inevitability. It is open to challenge and a strategy of resistance which may change our 'fate'. For Mills, 'drift' carries with it the first meaning of 'fate' — in this case innumerable decisions which have coalesced sometimes in unforeseen ways, and moved the world into cold war. 'Thrust' relates to actions which men or women take or refuse to take. Mills recognises that thrust and drift are intertwined and that both are leading towards the abyss of World War III. Yet, he argues, there is more scope for active intervention for peace than is commonly supposed — that thrust, as it were, can move against drift rather than with it. To seek to show how this can be done is both a challenge and an opportunity to cultural workmen. It is to claim a role for reason in responding to the unparalleled risks now facing humanity.

At the heart of Mills's position is the view that as war has become total — that is to say we now have the means with which to extinguish the human species and the planet — so it becomes absurd. There are no gains that would compensate for war or justify it since the end is annihilation. It is beyond reason. Distinctions between strategic and tactical weapons, between civilian and military populations are obsolete and the idea of civil defence is a black farce. Yet preparations for war continue on a massive scale as the vicious, deadly circle spirals on. We seek to avoid extinction by threatening each other with it. And in this world not of paradox but contradiction preparation for war is defined as a technological and administrative matter, a 'necessity' which is, as it were, 'beyond politics'; and peace is a controversial, worrying, divisive, 'political' word. What we are settling for in not questioning or challenging the conventional wisdom of deterrence is the simplification of known catastrophe. The immediate causes of World War III, Mills states, is the preparation for it.

Jonathan Schell, in a recent eloquent book, *The Fate of the Earth*, has summed the matter up thus: 'This is the circularity at the core of the nuclear deterrence doctrine: we seek to avoid our self-extinction by threatening to perform the act. According to this logic, it is almost as though if we stopped threatening ourselves with extinction, the extinction would occur' [83].

What then is to be done? Mills sees a public role for intellectual craftsmen. Having recognized the absurdity and danger of the present situation, the task is to offer alternatives. This is by definition a radical position in that it involves breaking out of the cold war ideology, rather than adjusting to it or merely trimming it. This is a strategy of resistance and an oppositional stance which seeks to reverse the present thrust of action. Not to do so, not to challenge the monopoly of cold war thinking, is to be in default of one's intellectual and political responsibility to work for peace. Moreover, although he is bitterly critical of the power elite in the USA and the USSR, he recognizes that if they could be persuaded to think otherwise, their great power is precisely what puts them in a position to make peace.

For this reason, Mills maintains, 'it is now sociologically realistic, morally fair and politically imperative to make demands upon men of power and to hold them responsible for specific courses of events' [84]. What he looks for is a world of peaceful competition and the co-existence of differently organized societies, a world in which information flows more freely, cultural and scientific exchanges develop with scope for open communication and independent dissent, and in which proper and urgent attention is given to responding to world poverty. This last point, although not central to the focus of the book is nevertheless strongly stated. American foreign policy, he thinks, too often works with an image of neutralists, pacifists and leftists controlled by conspiratorial troublemakers under direct orders from Moscow and Peking. This is not a realistic way of responding to global concerns: 'What matters today is how a world of properly developing societies can be built out of the impoverished *and* out of the overdeveloped monstrosities that now pass for human societies. And the first and continuing means to that end is negotiation' [85].

Mills does offer a number of guidelines for the USA upon which an alternative policy for peace could proceed. It is instructive to read them some twenty years later. They include: the recognition by the USA of China and all other communist states; an embargo on all arms shipments to the Middle East, Latin America, South East Asia and Africa; encourage the European nations to disarm unilaterally; the stopping of all nuclear tests; a unilateral decision to cease production of nuclear weapons and an announced policy for reducing the present stockpile; the abandonment of all military bases and installations outside the USA; entering into negotiations with the Soviet Union in the light of these stated initiatives. To those who would dismiss such an approach as utopian, Mills's reply is that it is infinitely preferable to the crackpot realism that currently prevails. Whatever the risks, they are not the risks of total annihilation.

Mills looks explicitly for disengagement in Central Europe and an all-European neutralization as a crucial means towards world disarmament. The present European peace movement is without question very much in the spirit of Mills's thinking on this issue.

The Causes of World War III is the foremost example of Mills's work in the prophetic mode. Yet it is the prophet calling for the politics of responsibility rather than irrational declamation. The prophet seeks to unmask the irresponsible pretensions of the powerful and to insist that the 'fate' that crackpot realism has in store for us can be transcended. The prophet calls others to the task of resurrecting the central goal of Western humanism — the audacious control by reason of man's fate. If the prophet speaks with an urgent and angry voice it is because human existence itself is at stake. Nevertheless, it is the voice of reason, which calls for a rational response and a commitment to the task of overcoming public apathy, indifference and elite irresponsibility. In the midst of the Cold War Mills was still a child of the Enlightenment.

2.10 MILLS AND THE CLASSIC TRADITION

The classic sociological tradition is a central part of the cultural tradition of Western civilization. The crisis of one is the crisis of the other; of all the spheres of Western culture, the classic tradition of sociology is the most directly relevant to those areas where culture and politics come now to such a terrifying point of intersection .... Such a tradition may be surpassed by political authority, it may also be diverted by those institutional and academic trends that form the climate of cultural work. It may be suppressed by the default of those who ought to be practicing it. [86]

This passage from *Images of Man* expresses clearly the high regard that Mills had for the sociological tradition. For him it was a great cultural and intellectual resource. Its existence could not be taken for granted and the task of the contemporary sociologist was to ensure that it was a living tradition. That the tradition should be threatened by those who saw the social sciences as disreputable or discomforting is understandable. That it should be neglected by social scientists themselves was more surprising and greatly to their discredit. Yet what was at stake was not some misplaced piety of ancestor worship. Rather it was the continuing stimulus to conceptual thought about society and modes of social reflection and social enquiry. The mark of writers in this tradition is that they ask and pursue questions about whole societies, the men and women who built them, and the nature of social change. Models of society are provided in and through which, for example, theories of stratification, capitalism, socialism and the relation of the individual to society are elaborated.

Why should this matter? Mills offers answers which intermingle the personal, the political and the cultural. They revolve around a humanistic view of sociology as a form of consciousness.

Reading sociology should increase our awareness of the imperial reach of social worlds into the intimacies of our very self. Such awareness, of course, is the cultural goal of all

learning as well as of much art. For all humanistic disciplines,
if properly cultivated, help us to transcend the moral sloth and
the intellectual rigidities that constitute most of everyday life
in every society of which we know, [87]

The transcendent element in sociology derives from Western
culture but also serves as a critique of it. The intellectual freedom which
it represents can also be viewed socially as a vehicle of cultural libera-
tion. To ignore, betray or attempt to abolish this activity is to injure
the body politic and to devalue the role of reason in human affairs.
This, in Mills's view, is why under tyranny sociology is among the first
of the cultural disciplines to be either abolished or turned into the uses
of an unfree ideology. To reflect, keep alive and extend the social
science tradition, as Mills understands it, is to be involved in a cultural
struggle. It is a struggle against those who by political means want to
blunt its critical edge, those who by economic means want to buy it off,
and those who with misplaced professionalism emasculate their own
heritage.

In *Images of Man* Mills illustrates, in a book of readings, how he
sees the classic tradition exemplified in a variety of contributors. From
the European scene he draws on Spencer, Marx, Engels, Durkheim,
Weber, Simmel, Michels, Mosca, Pareto and Mannheim. From American
sources (some of whom had lived in Europe also) he cites Schumpeter,
Veblen, Lippmann, Thomas and Znaniecki. This listing makes clear
that the classic tradition is not bounded by tight disciplinary considerations of what is sociological. Mills tends to use the terms sociology and
social science interchangeably. This is not done for reasons of disciplinary imperialism — almost the reverse. Professionally defined boundaries matter less than the substantive concern of writers to grapple
with the relationships between history and biography in society.
Indeed, the ability to do this well is one definition of the sociological
imagination. In Mills's view this promotes a more general social consequences: 'It is also the fact that their intellectual problems are relevant
to the public issues of their times and to the private troubles of individual men and women. More than that — they have helped to define
more clearly the issues and the troubles and the intimate relations
between the two' [88]. This is precisely the theme which pervades
The Sociological Imagination and to which we now turn.

The distinction between private troubles and public issues, noted
in the above quotation, may be connected to another distinction
between milieux and structure which we have already encountered in
Character and Social Structure. The private experience of difficulties

and anxieties at the level of common sense awareness is something which takes place, with its own reality at the level of milieux. But to explain why such experiences occur, Mills argues, we have to embark upon an institutional analysis. Hence questions of unemployment, war, marriage problems, and the experienced difficulties of urban life have to be examined within a context that sees the social-psychological reality as rooted in specific, historically formed social structures. Establishing linkages between private troubles in a variety of milieux and public issues in particular societies is an exercise which demands sociological imagination.

The reason for the polemical approach taken in *The Sociological Imagination* is that Mills felt strongly that the promise of the classic tradition had been betrayed by many contemporary American sociologists. He probably overstated his case, but this was presumably part of the shock tactics designed to challenge and provoke — which it did.

There was first an attack on what Mills termed 'grand theory'. This turns out essentially to be an attack on Talcott Parsons, not the Parsons of *The Structure of Social Action,* whom Mills had respectfully acknowledged in his earlier writings, but the Parsons of *The Social System.* With extended quotations from that book he derides Parsons's prose and offers his own translations in more down-to-earth language. Given Parsons's pre-eminent position in American sociology at that time, this was, to say the least, irreverent; and no doubt that was what some up-and-coming Young Turks liked about it.

Mills suggests that Parsons has 'fetishized his Concepts'. This has led to a monolithic model of society which has limited the ways in which the problem of social order is to be understood, has understated the role of power in social life and ignored the need to analyse social structures in historical perspective. That is why he claims that one *Behemoth* (which we have earlier discussed) is worth twenty *Social Systems* in advancing the social sciences. Naturally he is not arguing against theory, let alone large-scale studies of society. The contrasting approach which Mills advocates is in fact to be clearly seen in *Character and Social Structure* which we have earlier examined in some detail.

Much of Mills's attack here was well directed. At the same time, not all Parsons's work was as fruitless or as badly written as Mills suggests. In particular he wrote a number of essays on sociological topics which were much more elegant in style and more closely connected to the real world. These included, as it happens, essays on fascism and on German social structure, which Mills neglects to mention despite his enthusiastic reference to Neumann's *Behemoth* [89] .

Counterpoised against the fetishism of the Concept is the tyranny of The Method as evidenced in what Mills designates 'abstracted empiricism'. True to form, Mills attacks the king of the methodologists, Paul Lazarsfeld. If the grand theorists have a monolithic conceptual framework, the abstracted empiricists have a monolithic view about the nature of the scientific method. 'The style of social research I have called abstracted empiricism often seems to consist of efforts to re-state and adopt *philosophies* of *natural* science in such a way as to form a program and a canon for work in social science' [90]. Not only does Mills question the notion that there is one method for doing natural science but he also argues that, in practice, social scientists who take this view end up with methodological inhibitions. In the event 'theory' turns out to be the statistical manipulation of empirical data and method the statistical ritual whereby the 'variables' are defined and inter-related.

Mills is not arguing against the use of statistical procedures in social science. He is complaining that, in practice, the abstracted empiricists proceed to conduct trivial studies which are psychologistic in orientation and lacking in any sense of connection with the wider social structure. Their lack of epistemological awareness (and recall here Mills's own grounding in the sociology of knowledge) leads them to a pseudo-precision: 'If you have ever seriously studied for a year or two, some thousand hour-long interviews, carefully coded and punched, you will have begun to see how very malleable the realm of 'fact' may really be.' [91]. The end result is scattered information about scattered individuals in scattered milieux. Because no reflective attempt is made to relate milieux to historically located social structures no real progress can be made. The over-reliance on the standard interview and the sample survey, as a manageable means of collecting and operationalizing data leads, in Mills's view, to a truncated vision of social science with a built-in tendency to trivialization.

Does Mills over-state his case against Lazarsfeld? *The Language of Social Research*, edited by Lazarsfeld and Rosenberg, stands as a basic reference here and, taken as a whole, it does give a broader perspective on social analysis than Mills gives it credit for. In any case it can certainly be usefully consulted as a check against Mills's claims [92]. Paul Lazarsfeld's more recent essay, 'Working with Merton', might also be borne in mind [93]. The Lazarsfeld—Merton partnership produced, for example some innovative work in the mass media, of which Mills was well aware. In the process of this work interviewing techniques were developed which were sensitive to the different 'meanings' elicited from respondents. About Robert Merton there is a strange silence in *The*

Sociological Imagination. Hence there is no discussion of his book *Mass Persuasion* or of his seminal essay 'Patterns of Influence: Local and Cosmopolitan Influentials' [94]. Both of these studies came out of the Bureau of Applied Social Research. Lazarsfeld, it might be added, did much to help the Frankfurt School in exile during their New York sojourn — both personally and intellectually. Although there were serious disagreements from time to time, Lazarsfeld was very supportive, which suggests some proper caution in any considered evaluation of his intellectual stance [95].

Mills, however, has a general case to make. The dual pre-eminence of the grand theorists and the abstracted empiricists in American social science, represented, in his judgement, the abdication of the proper concerns of classic social science and it is this he deplores as a betrayal of 'the promise'.

The picture Mills paints of American social science in the 1940s and 1950s is a bleak one. There is the grand theory which simply does not connect with substantive problems. The effect is to provide ideological support for the status quo, since any kind of critique is not possible. There is the bureaucratization of the research institutes. Not only does this lead to a technician's view of social science but it becomes a vehicle of 'illiberal practicality'. That is to say, research is client-oriented and provides information for those who can afford to pay for it. The client defines the problem and the social scientist advises. Consequently, the idea that the social scientists has a responsibility to a wider public or does work that has general political relevance tends to get lost. Moreover, the older tradition of 'liberal practicality' among social scientists has lost its vigour. Their work, because it has not been sufficiently analytic — going beyond the study of 'troubles' — has been, for the most part, incorporated into the administrative liberalism of the welfare state. One way or another, social scientists have become the servants of power.

Mills does have a programmatic view as to what should be done. He argues for a position in which social scientists should collaborate in comparative and historically informed studies of social structures.

> Comparative and historical study are very deeply involved with each other. You cannot understand the under-developed, the Communist, the capitalist political economies as they exist in the world today by flat, timeless comparisons. You must expand the temporal reach of your analysis. To understand and to explain the comparative facts as they lie before you today, you must know the historical phases and the historical

reasons for varying rates and varying directions of development and lack of development [96].

Again, reference should be made back to *Character and Social Structure*
to understand more fully what Mills understands by this [97].

All this, however, is not simply a celebration of the pleasures of
contemplation and of the pursuit of knowledge for knowledge's sake.
Sociology is a form of consciousness. It is a product of the enlightenment, as were the two developed ideologies of liberalism and socialism.
However, in Mills's view both of these ideologies — which in their
different ways stressed the close relationship between the application of
human reason to social life and the growth of human freedom — have
collapsed as adequate explanations of the world and our part in it.
This leads him to write, rather dramatically, about the emergence of
The Fourth Epoch, in which reason and freedom are threatened in
capitalist and communist societies. This, therefore, places a special
obligation on social scientists, as co-heirs of the Enlightenment, to
apply critical thought so that the humanist values of reason and freedom may be recalled and applied to new social structures. Behind this,
and plainly stated by Mills, is a moral injunction:

> The moral and intellectual promise of social science is that
> freedom and reason will remain cherished values, that they
> will be used seriously and consistently and imaginatively in the
> formulation of problems. But this also is the political promise
> of what is loosely called Western culture. Within the social
> sciences, political crises and intellectual crises of our time
> coincide: serious work in either sphere is also work in the
> other .... Any contemporary political restatement of liberal
> and socialist goals must include as central the idea of a society
> in which all men would become men of substantive reason,
> whose independent reasoning would have structural conse-
> quences for their societies, its history, and thus for their own
> life fates. [98]

From that perspective and with a sense of urgency Mills calls upon
social scientists to take part in formulating, expressing and living a
'politics of truth'. They must themselves recover confidence in their
own capacity to reason. Guided by such values, some may serve as
advisers to those in power; others may work independently, analysing
structural trends and the public issues and private troubles to which
they give rise. In this way they would direct their work to those in
power as well as serve as educators of a range of 'publics'. Whether such
attempts to raise the level of public awareness will suffice to implement

the values of reason and freedom, and above all save the world from a self-destructive nuclear holocaust, cannot be known. Mills is rather pessimistic. But for him this is a challenge which it is preferable to face rather than passively accept a 'fate' determined by others. We are at this point as close as we are ever likely to get to understanding Mills's own vocabulary of motivation.

3

Conclusion:
a Key Sociologist?

> What does this solitary horseman — who is in part prophet, in part a teacher, in part a scholar, and in part a rough-tongued brawler — a sort of Joe McCarthy of sociology, full of wild accusations and gross inaccuracies, bullying manners, harsh words, and shifting grounds — want of sociology? [1]

The above quotation is taken from a review by Edward Shils of *The Sociological Imagination*. Written by a leading member of the American sociological establishment, it conveys something of the mixture of hostility, contempt and rancour with which Mills was regarded in some circles. Evidently, Shils needed no lessons from Mills in vituperation. To call Mills a sort of Joe McCarthy of sociology is an ugly insult in the context of that period of American history, that one can only wonder at Shils's lack of restraint and civility.

To read Shils's review is to understand something of the outrage and scandal Mills must have caused in the profession. Mills is portrayed in the image of a burly cowpuncher, riding up, from Texas to Columbia via Wisconsin. He reads Kafka, Trotsky and Weber as he rides onwards, meets a few people on his travels and writes an angry book. How can one take seriously such unassimilated, self-taught people, Shils seems to ask. Yet, by the end of the review, having dismissed Mills, he then goes on to denigrate sociology's present accomplishments and to claim that the sociological imagination could indeed 'provide an open pattern of thought, a realistic sensibility which could give guidance to our cognitive response to our society. It could be a general set of pointers indicating the significant aspects of situations, the range of possibilities and within that range, what is more likely and what is less likely to occur' [2]. This is precisely what Mills had argued in *The Sociological Imagination*. For Shils it was, one concludes, the wrong man speaking in the wrong tone of voice.

Other contemporaries also found themselves able to add insinuation to insult. Lipset and Smelser combined their talents for the benefit of British sociologists to offer their professional advice about the standing and activities of Mills:

> In any article discussing major trends in American sociology designed for publication in England it is clearly necessary to discuss C. Wright Mills for he seems to have became an intellectual hero to a youthful section of the British political community. It must be reported, however, that he has little importance for contemporary American sociology, although his books are bestsellers outside the field and are widely hailed in certain political circles. A book has already appeared sympathetically discussing his work by the editor of the theoretical organ of one of our smaller but better-known political parties .... But if Mr. Mills cuts himself off from the sociological fraternity he retains important outlets of expression from a more popular and commercial media and thus manages to influence the outside world's image of sociology. [3]

How unpleasant it all is — a nod here, a wink there justifying the dismissive put-down. Yet time passes. Lipset in recent years is able to cite Mills with approval. For example, in his essay 'Social Structure and Social Change', we are told with reference to *The Sociological Imagination* that Mills stood out almost alone among the prominent figures in the field — so he was a prominent figure after all — as a critic of the dominant orientations in modern sociology. This, it is pointed out, makes him an early exponent of the sociology of sociology [4]. Elsewhere Lipset has made a measured reference to Mills's discussion of the social role of the intellectual [5].

In a similar vein Daniel Bell has characterized Mills as an exponent of 'vulgar sociology' [6]. He complains that, in much of Mills's writing, points are not argued or developed, only asserted and re-asserted and that this really comes down to a strategy of rhetoric. Included in this strategy is the invocation of History. Bell objects to Mills describing the 'end of ideology' or 'the working class as a historical agency' as being historically outmoded. 'Does one accept events on the basis of inevitability or desirability? Mills never addresses himself to such questions. He stands simply as the caretaker of the dustbin of History' [7]. Bell protests too much. The curious thing is that in his end of ideology thesis he is the one who is telling us that the old ideologies are dead, or, as he might have put it, historically outmoded. Moreover, in his later work on post-industrial societies he singularly fails to come to grips with the issue of inevitability in social change. We are left unsure as to the status of his predictions about the future [8].

A comment of a slightly different order about Mills's sociology is to be found in Friedrich's study, *A Sociology of Sociology*:

> The paradigmatic fire that Mills kindled clearly warmed the sociological imagination of many of his confreres. It may, however, have served to consume him as well. The polemical nature of his later works, the squandering of his sociological talents on ideological outbursts, his readiness to condone the naked use of power all bespoke an intensity that saw force as the ultimate arbiter among men. [9]

Clearly there is a measure of appreciation of Mills's work in this judgement. However, the reference to Mills's view on the role of power should be questioned. It underlines a view of Mills as a neo-Machiavellian, who not only drew upon elite theorists in his work but also shared their cynical views about the use of power. Mills always made plain that he did not share their political perspective, particularly their tendency to disparage democracy.

In support of his view that Mills condoned the naked use of power, Friedrich cites a part sentence in *The Sociological Imagination* where we read: 'In the end, if the end comes, we just have to beat those who disagree with us over the head' [10]. Now this is said in the context of pointing out that in the last resort the final form of power is coercion. The whole thrust of his argument is, however, to hope that such an end is seldom reached and to plead for the role of reason in human affairs to prevent such an eventuality. An awareness that coercion is the last resort, is, for Mills, the ground for seeking rational alternatives, not an advocacy of the practice. The question is rather how can we envisage social orders in which those who have the means of killing or of incarcerating those with whom they disagree do not do so.

In noting the hostile, sometimes bitter, criticisms of Mills, we are reminded of what a controversial figure he was in his own lifetime. We do not need to over-compensate by making exaggerated claims on his behalf. In the body of this text we have already, by way of critical exposition, attempted a judicious appraisal of the range of his work. When all the reservations have been made and caveats entered, we offer the firm view that he should indeed be considered a key sociologist. In doing so there is no point in entering the competitive stakes and describing him as 'the greatest sociologist the United States has ever produced' [11]. Candy floss superlatives are neither here nor there. There are some things, however, which by way of conclusion we can say for him.

First, his fusion of American pragmatism and European sociology did lead to innovative work in the sociology of knowledge. This applies both to his substantive study *Sociology and Pragmatism* and also to his epistemological work on the problem of truth and validity in sociological enquiry. Mills and Merton stand as two leading figures and, to some extent, interacting exponents of the sociology of knowledge. Both of them mediate and develop Mannheim's work.

Secondly, proper tribute can be made to the range of studies which he accomplished in what was, after all, quite a short working life. Each of the studies has strengths and weaknesses, as we have sought to show. But they do show a range of interests which are held together by a pre-eminent concern to understand American society and its place in world affairs. In most of his work Mills has in mind a reading public beyond the boundaries of professional social science. Most of his work is accessible without being condescending to the general reader and that is no mean achievement.

Thirdly, and of considerable importance, there is the intellectual stimulus which his work has given to others. This is of various kinds. There are what we may call the routine scholarly references to Mills's work found in the literature. Simply by way of an instance we mention Dahrendorf's *Class and Class Conflict in an Industrial Society*, which refers to Mills's very balanced account of views about 'the new middle class' [12]. More generally, Mills's discussion of power has reverberated through the sociological literature. His critique of 'romantic pluralism' has been taken up by a number of writers who stress the continuing inequalities which exist in modern societies. Again, the treatment of power as sometimes non-observable, hidden, and manipulative, affecting people without their knowing it, has also been taken up. The seminal discussion in Steven Lukes's *Power* bears particular witness to this [13]. The affinities of Mills's analysis of institutional power and Gramsci's now well-known discussion of hegemony is worth noting here, although there is no clear reason for thinking that Mills was directly influenced by Gramsci's work [14].

Besides the general debate over the concept of power, there has been continuing discussion and research around the configuration identified as the military—industrial complex. The most useful single reference here is the collection of research papers, edited by Steven Rosen, *Testing the Theory of the Military-Industrial Complex* [15]. Rosen points out that the theory itself became part of the consciousness of every attentive student of politics and society. Reviewing the papers in his volume, Rosen concludes that the essential propositions of the theory have been sustained: 'it is remarkable how well it has withstood critical evaluation, some of it from an obviously sceptical perspective' [16].

The extent of Mills's intellectual influence among his contemporaries is well reflected in the collection of essays written in his honour and to his memory namely, *The New Sociology* and *Sociology on Trial* [17]. They also show the interest in his work manifested in Europe and Latin America, as well as in the United States. where he was not such an isolated figure as he sometimes supposed. The essays do not represent the birth of a Millsian school. Essentially they shared a concern that sociology might become a professionally closed, ossified discipline and warned against the dangers of a monolithic orthodoxy. As such they did encourage a critical approach to the study of society, without being linked to a new orthodoxy as to what constitutes the most adequate framework of analysis. They did, however, converge on a view that sociology should apply itself to studying the major movements of our time. One of the contributors, Peter Worsley, took this point up again in his book *The Third World* [18]. He cites Mills's warning on the twin dangers of grand theory and abstracted empiricism and argues that the question of under-development and the issue of nuclear war should stand high on the social science agenda.

Irving Horowitz did a very great deal to advance the claims of Mills's sociology. He edited *The New Sociology*, Mills's collected essays, *Power, Politics and People* and the posthumously published *Sociology and Pragmatism*. In each case there are introductory essays on Mills's work which are of great value. The influence of Mills has spilled over into Horowitz's own work. Simply by way of illustration mention might be made of his essay, 'Mainliners and Marginals: the Human Shape of Sociological Theory', which builds upon *The Sociological Imagination* in its discussion of the professionalization of sociology in the United States [19], and his books *Three Worlds of Development* and *The War Game* which take up two of Mills's substantive concerns [20].

Another writer with a close affinity to Mills was undoubtedly the late Alvin Gouldner. Gouldner came to define himself as a 'Marxist outlaw', by which he meant that even Marxism as a critical theory must be subject to critique. In *The Dialectic of Ideology and Technology* he writes: 'At its most fundamental level, my standpoint remains very much that of C. Wright Mills whose own radicalism and reflexivity was never expressed as a commitment to Marxism' [21]. Gouldner's *The Coming Crisis of Western Sociology* is very much in the tradition of Mills (with a very lengthy and much more considered discussion of Parsons). The book embodied a sharp attack on what he saw as the dominant forms of sociology in the USA and the USSR and was treated as a scandalous intervention in much the same way that *The Sociological Imagination* had been a decade earlier [22].

Mills was a controversial sociologist who lived, as we do, in difficult times. His work remains of value. To the emerging radical sociologists in the United States he became something of a heroic figure. In Europe his work was much discussed [23]. Whatever our overall judgement of his achievements he is a difficult person to ignore. We do not now have to answer Shils's question — what does he want of sociology. We can, with proper critical awareness, acknowledge what he has given.

Notes and References

Chapter 1 — THE MAKING OF CULTURAL WORKMAN

[1] Editorial Introduction to C. Wright Mills, *Sociology and Pragmatism*, Oxford University Press, 1966, p. 12.

[2] Cited by Irving Horowitz, in 'Mannheim's Wissenssoziologie und C. W. Mills' Soziologisches Wissen', in *Kölner Zeitschrift für Soziologie und Sozialpsychologie*, Sonderdruck aus Sonderheft 22/1980.

[3] Richard Gillam, 'White Collar from Start to Finish', in *Theory and Society*, **10**, 5, 1981.

[4] This and a little more biographical information can be found in Joseph A. Scimecca, *The Sociological Theory of C. Wright Mills*, Kennikat Press Corps, 1977, Chapter 2.

[5] C. Wright Mills (ed.) *Images of Man*, George Braziller, 1960, p. 13.

[6] Editorial Introduction to Thorstein Veblen, *The Theory of the Leasure Class*, Mentor, 1953, p. xix.

[7] Cited in *Images of Man*, op. cit., pp. 367–368.

[8] Ibid., p. 369.

[9] Horowitz, in *Sociology and Pragmatism*, op. cit., p. 12.

[10]   C. Wright Mills, *The Sociological Imagination,* Oxford University Press, 1959, p. 6.

[11]   *Sociology and Pragmatism,* op. cit., p. 330.

[12]   *The Sociological Theory of C. Wright Mills,* op. cit., p. 13.

[13]   Reprinted in C. Wright Mills, *Power, Politics and People,* Oxford University Press, p. 433.

[14]   Reprinted in *Power Politics and People,* op. cit., p. 454.

[15]   Ibid., p. 460.

[16]   Ibid., p. 468.

[17]   Derek L. Phillips, 'Epistemology and the Sociology of Knowledge: the contributions of Mannheim, Mills and Merton', in *Theory and Society,* **1**, 1, 59–88, 1974.

[18]   See Thomas S. Kuhn, *The Structure of Scientific Revolutions,* University of Chicago Press, 1962; Imre Lakatos and Alan Musgrave (eds.), *Criticism and the Growth of Knowledge,* Cambridge University Press, 1970.

[19]   Ernest Gellner, *Cause and Meaning in the Social Sciences,* Routledge and Kegan Paul, 1973; Steven Lukes, *Essays in Social Theory,* Macmillan, 1977.

[20]   'Situated Actions and Vocabularies of Motives', reprinted in *Power Politics and People,* op. cit., p. 443.

[21]   Hans Gerth, 'C. Wright Mills, 1916–1962', *Studies on the Left,* **2**, 3, 7–11.

[22]   Hans Gerth and C. Wright Mills (eds.), *From Max Weber,* Routledge & Kegan Paul, 1948, p. 72.

[23]   Ibid., p. 70.

[24]   Ibid., p. 64.

[25]   Ibid., p. 128.

[26]   See Max Weber, 'Class, Status, Party', in *From Max Weber,* op. cit., pp. 180–195.

[27]   For a famous critique of the professional sociologists see Alvin Gouldner, 'Anti-Minotaur: the Myth of a Value-Free Sociology', in Irving Horowitz (ed.), *The New Sociology,* Oxford University Press, 1964, pp. 196–217.

[28]   For the definitive discussion of the Frankfurt School see, Martin Jay, *The Dialectical Imagination,* Heinemann, 1973.

[29]   Robert S. Lynd and Helen Merrell Lynd, *Middletown in Transition,* Harcourt, Brace, 1937.

[30]   See 'The Social Life of a Modern Community', reprinted in *Power, Politics and People,* op. cit., pp. 39–52.

[31]   Foreword to R. A. Brady, *Business as a System of Power,* Columbia University Press, 1943, p. xii.

[32]   *The Sociological Imagination,* op. cit., p. 115.
[33]   Reprinted in Robert K. Merton, *Social Theory and Social Structure,* Free Press, 1957, pp. 456–488.
[34]   Ibid., p. 482.
[35]   See *Social Theory and Social Structure,* op. cit., pp. 85–117.
[36]   Reprinted in *Power, Politics and People,* op. cit., pp. 525–552.
[37]   Cited in Robert K. Merton, 'Structural Analysis in Sociology', in Peter M. Blau (ed.), *Approaches to the Study of Social Structure,* Open Books, 1976, p. 38.
[38]   The essay is reprinted in *Social Theory and Social Structure,* op. cit., pp. 509–528.
[39]   Paul Lazarsfeld, 'Working with Merton', in Lewis A. Coser (ed.), *The Idea of Social Structure. Papers in Honor of Robert K. Merton,* Harcourt, Brace, Jovanovich, 1975, pp. 36–66.
[40]   Reprinted in *Power, Politics and People,* op. cit., pp. 577–598.
[41]   Ibid., p. 586.
[42]   Cited in Herbert Aptheker, *The World of C. Wright Mills,* Marzoni and Minsell, 1960, p. 123.
[43]   Reprinted in *Power, Politics and People,* op. cit., pp. 553–567.
[44]   *Social Theory and Social Structure,* op. cit., pp. 3–16.
[45]   'Two Styles of Social Science Research, in *Power, Politics and People,* op. cit., p. 556.
[46]   Chaim Waxman, *The End of Ideology Debate,* Simon and Schuster, 1969.
[47]   Ibid., p. 102.
[48]   Ibid., p. 134.
[49]   'On Knowledge and Power', in *Power, Politics and People,* op. cit., p. 611.
[50]   *The Marxists,* Penguin, 1962. p. 13.
[51]   Reprinted in Talcott Parsons, *Essays in Sociological Theory,* Free Press, 1964, pp. 323–335.
[52]   Ibid., p. 335.
[53]   *The Marxists,* op. cit., pp. 97–98.
[54]   Ibid., p. 129.

Chapter 2 – The Intellectual Craftsman

[1]   *The Sociological Imagination,* op. cit., p. 224.
[2]   Ibid., p. 206.
[3]   Ibid., p. 213.

[4]   *Proceedings of the first annual meeting of the Industrial Rela-
      tions Research Society, 1948,* and cited in P. Blumberg, *Indus-
      trial Democracy: the Sociology of Participation,* Constable,
      1968, p. 45. See also, J. E. T. Eldridge, 'Sociological Imagina-
      tion and Industrial Life', in Malcolm Warner (ed.) *The Sociology
      of the Workplace,* Allen & Unwin, 1973, pp. 274–286.

[5]   'Man in the Middle: the Designer', in *Power, Politics and People,*
      op. cit., p. 386.

[6]   Richard Gillam, op. cit., p. 2.

[7]   *White Collar,* Oxford University Press, 1956, p. 166.

[8]   *The Power Elite,* Oxford University Press, 1959, pp. 186–187.

[9]   *Sociology and Pragmatism,* op. cit., p. 210.

[10] Ibid., p. 227.

[11] Ibid., p. 242.

[12] Ibid., p. 268.

[13] Ibid., p. 331.

[14] Ibid., p. 413.

[15] Hans Gerth and C. Wright Mills, *Character and Social Structure,*
      Routledge & Kegan Paul, 1954, p. xiii.

[16] Ibid., p. 32.

[17] Ibid., p. 14.

[18] Dell Hymes, *Foundations in Sociolinguistics. An Ethnographic
      Approach,* Tavistock, 1974.

[19] *Character and Social Structure,* op. cit., p. 114.

[20] Ibid., p. 123.

[21] Ibid., p. 297.

[22] Ibid., p. 353.

[23] Ibid., p. 377.

[24] Ibid., p. 404.

[25] Reprinted in J. E. T. Eldridge (ed.) *Max Weber. The Interpre-
      tation of Social Reality,* Nelson, 1972, pp. 254–275.

[26] *Character and Social Structure,* op. cit., p. 472.

[27] Ibid., p. 460.

[28] *The New Men of Power,* Harcourt Brace, 1948, p. 9.

[29] Ibid., p. 15.

[30] Ibid., p. 18.

[31] Ibid., p. 18.

[32] Ibid., p. 24.

[33] Ibid., p. 25.

[34] Ibid., p. 34.

[35] Ibid., pp. 251–252.

[36] Ibid., p. 261.

[37]   Ibid., p. 291.

[38]   Ibid., p. 108.

[39]   *White Collar*, op. cit., p. xviii.

[40]   Ibid., p. xv.

[41]   M. Crozier, *The World of the Office Worker*, Chicago University Press, 1971, p. 27.

[42]   *White Collar*, op. cit., p. 323.

[43]   Richard Gillam, 'White Collar from Start to Finish', op. cit., p. 9.

[44]   *White Collar*, op cit., pp. xvi–xvii.

[45]   Gillam, op. cit., p. 12.

[46]   *White Collar*, op. cit., p. xvi.

[47]   Ibid., p. 349.

[48]   Ibid., p. 335.

[49]   Ibid., p. 300.

[50]   *The Power Elite*, op. cit., p. 324.

[51]   W. Spinrad, 'The Socio-Political Orientations of C. Wright Mills', *Brtish Journal of Sociology*, xvii, I, 46-59, 1966.

[52]   *The Sociological Imagination*, op. cit., p. 200.

[53]   These essays are reprinted in *Power, Politics and People*, op. cit., pp. 53–71 and 170–178.

[54]   Ibid., p. 174.

[55]   Ibid., p. 177.

[56]   For a comparison between Mills and Riesman see, W. Kornhauser, ' "Power Elite" or "Veto Group",' in Reinhard Bendix and Seymour Martin Lipset (eds.), *Class, Status and Power*, Routledge & Kegan Paul, 1967, pp. 210–218.

[57]   See, for example, Ralph Miliband, *The State in Capitalist Society*, Weidenfeld and Nicolson, 1969; and Herbert Aptheker, op. cit.

[58]   *The Power Elite*, op. cit., pp. 360–361.

[59]   Reprinted in Talcott Parsons, *Structure and Process in Modern Societies*, Free Press, 1964, pp. 199–225.

[60]   Ibid., p. 205.

[61]   Cited in Scimecca, op. cit., p. 11.

[62]   Miliband, op. cit., pp. 136–137.

[63]   Harold R. Gracey and C. Arnold Anderson, Review of *The Power Elite, Kentucky Law Journal*, **46,** 309, 1958.

[64]   Daniel Bell, 'Is there a Ruling Class in America? *The Power Elite* Reconsidered', reprinted in *The End of Ideology*, Free Press, 1962, pp. 47–74.

[65]   *The Power Elite*, op. cit., p. 184.

[66] Bell, op. cit., p. 47.
[67] William Domhoff, *The Higher Circles*, Vintage, 1971.
[68] Aptheker, op. cit., pp. 24–25.
[69] Robert Blauner, *Racial Oppression in America*, Harper & Row, 1972, p. 23.
[70] C. Wright Mills, Clarence Senior and Rose K. Goldsen, *Puerto Rican Journey*, Oxofrd University Press, 1950.
[71] Ibid., p. 85.
[72] Blauner, op. cit., especially Chapters 1–3.
[73] *Puerto Rican Journey*, op. cit., pp. 43–44.
[74] C. Wright Mills, *Listen Yankee. The Revolution in Cuba*, Secker & Warburg, 1960, p. 8.
[75] John Dunn *Modern Revolutions*, Cambridge University Press, 1972, p. 213.
[76] C. Wright Mills, *The Causes of World War III*, Ballantine Books, 1960, p. 22.
[77] Ibid., p. 171.
[78] *The Church and the Bomb*, the report of a working party under the chairmanship of the Bishop of Salisbury, Hodder & Stoughton, 1982.
[79] *Causes of World War III*, op. cit., pp. 178–179.
[80] Bertrand Russell, *Has Man a Future?*, Penguin, 1961.
[81] Cited in Carroll W. Pursell Jr. (ed.), *The Military-Industrial Complex*, Harper, 1972, pp. 206–207.
[82] Reprinted in Edward Thompson *et al.*, *Exterminism and Cold War*, Verso, 1983, pp. 1–33.
[83] Jonathan Schell, *The Fate of the Earth*, Cape, 1982, p. 201.
[84] *The Causes of World War III*, op. cit., p. 116.
[85] Ibid., p. 121.
[86] *Images of Man*, op. cit., p. 9.
[87] Ibid., p. 17.
[88] Ibid., p. 4.
[89] In *Essays in Sociological Theory*, op. cit.
[90] *The Sociological Imagination*, op. cit., p. 57.
[91] Ibid., p. 72.
[92] Paul F. Lazarsfeld and Morris Rosenberg (eds.), *The Language of Social Research*, Free Press, 1955.
[93] In Lewis A. Coser (ed.), op. cit., pp. 35–66.
[94] Reprinted in *Social Theory and Social Structure*, op. cit., pp. 387–420.
[95] See Martin Jay, *The Dialectical Imagination*, op. cit.
[96] *The Sociological Imagination*, op. cit., pp. 150–151.

[97]   *Character and Social Structure,* op. cit., especially Part Four.
[98]   *The Sociological Imagination,* op. cit., pp. 173–174.

Chapter 3 – CONCLUSION: A KEY SOCIOLOGIST?

[1]   Edward Shils, 'Imaginary Sociology', *Encounter,* **14,** 78, 1960.
[2]   Ibid., p. 81.
[3]   S. M. Lipset and N. Smelser, 'Change and Controversy in Recent American Sociology', *British Journal of Sociology,* **XII,** 1, 50, 1961.
[4]   In P. Blau (ed.) *Approaches to the Study of Social Structure,* Open Books, 1976, pp. 172–209.
[5]   S. M. Lipset and A. Basu, 'Intellectual Types and Political Roles', in Lewis A. Coser, op. cit., pp. 433–470.
[6]   Reprinted in *Sociological Journeys,* Heinemann, 1980, pp. 138–143.
[7]   Ibid., p. 141.
[8]   See J. E. T. Eldridge, Review Article, *British Journal of Industrial Relations,* xii, 2, 303–307, 1974.
[9]   Robert Friedrich, *A Sociology of Sociology,* Free Press, 1970, p. 148.
[10]   *The Sociological Imagination,* op. cit., p. 77.
[11]   Irving Horowitz, in *Power, Politics and People,* op. cit., p. 20.
[12]   Ralph Dahrendorf, *Class and Class Conflict in an Industrial Society,* Routledge & Kegan Paul, 1959, p. 54.
[13]   Steven Lukes, *Power, A Radical View,* Macmillan, 1974.
[14]   There is a brief reference in *The Marxists,* op. cit., p. 97.
[15]   Steven Rosen (ed.), *Testing The Theory of the Military–Industrial Complex,* D. C. Heath, 1973.
[16]   Ibid., p. 25.
[17]   Irving Horowitz (ed.), *The New Sociology,* Oxford University Press, 1964. Maurice Stein and Arthur Vidich (eds.), *Sociology on Trial,* Prentice-Hall, 1963.
[18]   Peter Worsley, *The Third World,* Weidenfeld & Nicolson, 1967.
[19]   Irving Horowitz, *Professing Sociology,* Aldine, 1968, pp. 195–220.
[20]   Irving Horowitz, *Three Worlds of Development,* Oxford University Press, 1966; *The War Game,* 1963.
[21]   Alvin Gouldner, *The Dialectic of Ideology and Technology,* Macmillan, 1976, p. xiv.

[22]   See the *American Journal of Sociology*, July, 1972, and Gould-
       ner's response in *For Sociology*, Penguin, 1973, especially
       pp. 82–170.
[23]   For the British case in particular, see John Eldridge, *Recent
       British Sociology*, Macmillan, 1980.

Suggestions for Further Reading

First, for convenience, here is a consolidated list of Mills's own books:

From Max Weber: Essays in Sociology
    edited and translated with H. Gerth. Routledge and Kegan Paul,
    1948.
There is an introductory essay.

The New Men of Power
    co-author Helen Schneider. Harcourt Brace, 1948.

The Puerto Rican Journey
    co-authors Clarence Senior and Rose K. Goldsen. Oxford University
    Press, 1950.

White Collar, Oxford University Press.

Character and Social Structure
    co-author H. Gerth, Routledge and Kegan Paul, 1954.

The Power Elite, Oxford University Press.

The Sociological Imagination, Oxford University Press, 1959.

The Causes of World War III, Ballantine Books, 1960 (revised edition).

Listen Yankee: The Revolution in Cuba, Secker and Warburg, 1960.

Images of Man, edited and with an introductory essay, George Braziller,
    1960.

The Marxists. This is an extended commentary on a selection of Marxist and socialist writing. Penguin, 1962.

Power, Politics and People
  The collected essays of C. Wright Mills, edited by Irving Louis Horowitz, Oxford University Press, 1963. There is a good introductory essay by Horowitz and a very extensive bibliography of Mills's writings and reviews of his work. This is an important reference source.

Sociology and Pragmatism, edited and introduced by Irving Louis Horowitz, Oxford University Press, 1966.

Some useful general discussions of C. Wright Mills are to be found in the following:

Herbert Aptheker, *The World of C. Wright Mills,* Marzoni and Minsell, 1960. This is a critical appraisal written from a Marxist standpoint. It contains a summary of critical assessments from a variety of perspectives in the last chapter.

David Binns, *Beyond the Sociology of Conflict,* Macmillan, 1977. Chapter 6, C. Wright Mills: the Struggle to Make History, is well worth consulting. The critique again is from a Marxist standpoint.

R. P. Cuzzort, *Humanity and Modern Social Thought,* Holt, Rinehart and Winston, 1969. Chapter 7, The Sociologist in Anger: the Views of C. Wright Mills, is a useful text book summary of some of Mills's work.

Richard Gillam, White Collar from Start to Finish, *Theory and Society,* 10, 5, 1981. Not only is this a very authoritative account of *White Collar,* it also contains important references to other parts of Mills's work.

Joseph A. Scimecca, *The Sociological Theory of C. Wright Mills,* Kennikat Press Corps, 1977. Apart from the present book this is the only full length study of Mills's work.

Finally reference may be made to two collections of essays written in honour of C. Wright Mills:

Irving Horowitz, ed. *The New Sociology,* Oxford University Press, 1964. This remains an extremely useful source book and the international range of authors is a testimony to Mills's influence.

Maurice Stein and Arthur Vidich, eds. *Sociology on Trial,* Prentice-Hall, 1963.

Index

110923